SOUL MATTERS
for MEN

Wisdom & Inspiration
for the Most Important
Issues of Your Life

SOul
MATTERS
for MEN

A Division of Thomas Nelson Publishers
Since 1798

www.thomasnelson.com

Contents

Take Care of Your Soul

What good is it if someone gains the whole world—but loses their soul?

In our mad-dash, non-stop way of life, we too often forget about—or blatantly ignore—what matters most for our lives. But deep down, the simple truth that nothing—no achievements, no pleasures, no possessions—equals the value of the human soul, resonates in our inner being. Because what we most want for ourselves is to live our lives with significance and meaning. We long to be all that God created us to be.

If you have found yourself too busy and too distracted by the hundreds of things that clamor for your attention to seek nourishment for your soul; if you have been simply going through the motions of fulfilling God's best plans for your life; if you are ready to stop floating with the currents of a joyless and shallow society in order to see a remarkable difference in your life—and profoundly impact the lives of those around you—then *Soul Matters for Men* is for you.

Soul Matters for Men tackles almost fifty of the crucial life issues men face, weaving together poignant personal reflection questions, inspirational quotes, real life stories from others, God's promises, brief—but hard-hitting—Bible studies, practical life application ideas, and prayer starters to help you to discover for yourself how to let your soul take flight and soar!

We need to attend diligently to the state of our soul,
and to deal fervently and effectively with God about it.

JOHN OWEN

User's Guide

SOUL MATTERS FOR MEN *is easy to follow and use, but to maximize the benefit you get from this resource, here are a few quick ideas and suggestions for your consideration.*

TO THINK ABOUT

In any area of study, when we understand how a topic relates to our specific circumstances, we experience increased levels of interest, comprehension, and retention. When you ask yourself the questions with each topic, take your time and reflect on recent events in your own life.

LESSON FOR LIFE

These quick, hard-hitting, to-the-point Bible studies are not designed to provide you with everything you need to know and "all the answers" on each of the topics, but they are designed to stimulate your own thinking and discovery learning. You will enhance what is provided here when you take the extra time to look up all the Bible passages that are referenced.

"God Will" Promises

One of the ways our souls take flight is when we truly believe in our hearts that God is good and faithful. These life-changing promises have been embraced and experienced by men of faith for centuries and have stood the test of time. When one of the promises is particularly relevant to your life, take a few extra minutes to memorize the verse so it will always be close to your heart.

REAL LIFE

True life stories are an inspiring way to see how God is at work in the life of others. Some of these stories will be exactly what you need to make some important life changes and decisions. But you don't have to relate to every single person's story to discover dynamics that will help you experience God's presence more fully in your life.

ACTION

Not every Action Step found in *Soul Matters for Men* will be just right for you. But don't be afraid to stretch yourself and try something you would not normally think of on your own. Or let the ideas found with each soul matter prompt you to come up with an even better way to put truth into practice.

PRAYER

Let this brief prayer starter help you express your own requests, thanksgiving, and praise to God.

GROWING STRONGER THROUGH ADVERSITY

WHEN FACED WITH SETBACKS
AND OBSTACLES, GOD GIVES US THE GRACE
TO ACCOMPLISH SPECTACULAR THINGS.

*We shall draw from the heart of suffering itself
the means of inspiration and survival.*

WINSTON CHURCHILL

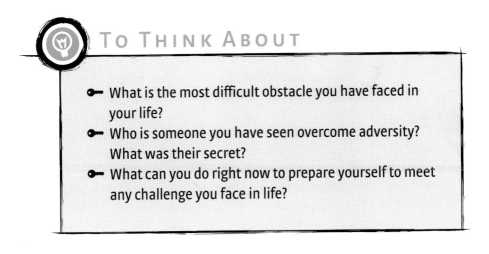

TO THINK ABOUT

- What is the most difficult obstacle you have faced in your life?
- Who is someone you have seen overcome adversity? What was their secret?
- What can you do right now to prepare yourself to meet any challenge you face in life?

LESSON FOR LIFE

Count It All Joy

BIBLE STUDY PASSAGE: ROMANS 8:10-39

My brothers and sisters, when you have many kinds of troubles, you should be full of joy, because you know that these troubles test your faith, and this will give you patience. Let your patience show itself perfectly in what you do. Then you will be perfect and complete and will have everything you need.

JAMES 1:2-4

No matter what our address, most of us live in a relatively healthy, secure, affluent society. Such conditions make it easy to feel a sense of privilege, a sense that we deserve only good things in our lives—a peaceful and comfortable existence.

Innocent men and women all over the world know no such comfort. In fact, living at the beginning of the third millennium since Christ's birth, there are more Christians martyred each year than in any previous decade of Christian history.

James, the brother of Jesus and the leader of the early church in Jerusalem, witnessed firsthand the horrors of persecution and hardship.

Yet he calls for his fellow believers to face all trials and tests with joy, faith, and optimism. He never asks for us to wish for hard times, but he does remind us that hard times— whether financial, physical, relational, or emotional— combined with faith, are opportunities for becoming a mature, spiritual person.

When you pass through the waters, I will be with you. When you cross rivers, you will not drown. When you walk through fire, you will not be burned, nor will the flames hurt you. This is because I, the Lord, am your God, the Holy One of Israel, your Savior.
Isaiah 43:2-3

REAL LIFE

Wannabe Lance Armstrong: A Real Winner

AS TOLD TO KATHERINE J. CRAWFORD

In April, six weeks after major cancer surgery and thirteen months after my initial cancer diagnosis, I sat in the oncologist's office for a follow-up visit. I looked and felt every bit of my sixty-five years. I had lost seventy pounds and my skin hung like a wrinkled white sheet.

As bad as I looked, I knew God had guided me through every step of my cancer journey. Psalm 139:16 says, "All the days planned for me were written in your book before I was one day old." I felt certain God had me in mind when He wrote that verse.

When I was first diagnosed with cancer, the oncologist had said I had little chance of survival. My wife didn't give up hope. She found a nutrition program and then eventually a cancer specialist to perform my surgery. Now I was waiting to find out what the future held for me.

When the oncologist entered the room, he smiled and said, "I don't know what you're doing in my cancer clinic, you old curmudgeon—I do believe you are cancer free."

I left the clinic wanting to believe the doctor, but I felt so weak and depressed. At my next checkup, the doctor suggested I bicycle to build my cardiovascular health. On our way out, I heard him to say to my wife, "Will you relax? He's doing great."

I bought a Raleigh ten-speed at a garage sale for eleven dollars. That first day, I rode a few blocks and then back to the house to collapse in a chair. Each day, I determined to ride further. That's when the Tour de France started.

One morning I called my wife at her office. "Look, if Lance can survive cancer and ride, so can I. Just call me a Lance Armstrong wannabe."

Each day I rooted for Lance on the Tour and studied more about bicycles. I wanted to understand the new racing equipment and aerodynamics. As I studied, I realized the Raleigh frame was not large enough for my height.

At a thrift store, I bought a Panasonic frame for seventeen dollars, took it home, and combined the two bikes. What a difference—the hills around our house became much easier. My next great challenge came in convincing my wife I needed a real racing bike.

It's been seven months since my surgery, and we now have a Bianchi bicycle in the front hall, a racing helmet on the newel post, jerseys hung on hooks, bike shoes in the closet, and my wife cheering from the sidelines.

I now weigh a solid 185 pounds, I'm tanned, and my legs are strong. I ride fifty miles at least three days a week and shorter sprints on the other days. While I'm out on my bike, I spend time in devotions, and each day I make an effort to share with someone how God miraculously brought me back from a terminal prognosis.

Maybe—just maybe—I'll race one of these days. I'm a wannabe Lance Armstrong: a real winner.

ACTION STEP

WHAT IS THE HARSHEST SITUATION YOU ARE FACING IN YOUR LIFE RIGHT NOW? GIVE SERIOUS THOUGHT AND PRAYER TO THE QUESTION OF HOW GOD WANTS YOU TO GROW AS A MAN THROUGH THIS ADVERSITY. HOW CAN YOU WORK WITH GOD TO GROW, TO BECOME A MORE COMPLETE PERSON?

PRAYER

Lord, protect me and my loved ones from evil people, from disease, from temptations when faced with hardship. Help me to become the man You have created me to be.

GOD'S PLAN FOR YOUR LIFE

ONE SIZE DOESN'T FIT ALL IN LIFE—
DISCOVER WHAT GOD'S BEST IS FOR YOU.

Walk boldly and wisely.
There is a hand above that will help you on.

PHILIP JAMES BAILEY

To Think About

- What are different ways you have discovered who you are and who you are meant to be thus far in your life?
- Do you feel you are accomplishing specifically what God has set forth for you to do?
- How would you answer the question: "What do you want to be when you grow up?"

LESSON FOR LIFE

PROMISES

God will—

Enlighten you
2 Samuel 22:29

Show you the way you
should go
Isaiah 48:17

Speak your name
John 10:14-15

Show you new truths
John 16:13

One Size Doesn't Fit All

BIBLE STUDY PASSAGE: 1 CORINTHIANS 1

*From Paul, an apostle of Christ Jesus by the will of God.
God sent me to tell about the promise of life that is in
Christ Jesus.*

2 TIMOTHY 1:1

One of the churches that St. Paul founded, the church at
Corinth, proved to be a particularly troublesome burden on his
heart. Yes, they were smart and sophisticated (1 Corinthians
4:10)—if you don't believe that, just ask them—but they had
lots of problems, most notably a spirit of divisiveness—

- *They argued over who the best leader was (1 Corinthians 1:12).*
- *They argued over who was most spiritual (1 Corinthians 3:3).*
- *They argued over what the most important gifts were (1
  Corinthians 12).*
- *They argued about the role of women in church services (1
  Corinthians 14:33-34).*
- *They even argued over whether Paul was worthy of respect (2
  Corinthians 10:10).*

Paul scolded them, shamed them, and even begged them to be united in love (1 Corinthians 1:10).   And he used their spirit of contentiousness as opportunity to teach them about God's plans for us.   He reminds the Corinthians that—

- *Each of us has unique gifts (1 Corinthians 12:28).*
- *Everyone's gifts are needed to complete the Body of Christ (1 Corinthians 12:12).*
- *We aren't to compare the value of our gifts (1 Corinthians 12:17).*
- *We aren't united because we are just like each other, but because we love each other (1 Corinthians 12:30-13:1).*

The good news for you is that God has made you one-of-a-kind unique—just like He has everyone else.   Your job is not to be like others, but to discover and fulfill God's giftings for you—and to affirm and support others in that same quest.

Have you been missing out on God's best for you by trying to please everyone else?

Anyone who has the gift of serving should serve. Anyone who has the gift of teaching should teach. Whoever has the gift of encouraging others should encourage. Whoever has the gift of giving to others should give freely.   Anyone who has the gift of being a leader should try hard when he leads. Whoever has the gift of showing mercy to others should do so with joy.
Romans 12:7-8

REAL LIFE

Seeking Forward Motion

KEN CLIFTON

Forward progress is forward progress. When I reflect upon how far our family has come, I am grateful I learned that lesson. However, that forward progress might come in ways that you don't expect. For us, that was the case.

Seven years ago, we declared bankruptcy. It seemed that one thing went wrong after another—the car got stolen; more than one job fell through; our move across state lines made our Medicaid coverage of my daughter's birth null, leaving us with thousands of dollars of debt. After many months of avoiding creditors, we finally filed bankruptcy papers.

All of the debt problems and attempts to get into a higher income were affected by my job history and experience level, which in turn affected my chances for getting the right job. It was a mess. After a few more years of shuffling between jobs and job interviews, I finally joined the military to solve our financial problems. This helped for a while, even though I was totally unhappy with my job choice. Then, I got injured. In desperation, we had to come up with another solution.

Here I should point out that my wife is a highly driven individual. Even when she was at home, she was the busiest homemaker on the planet. She even worked in management for a few years, stopping only to go to college for a business management degree while I was injured in the military.

After my injury and news of my future departure from the service, my wife and I took a step back and considered our options. What I discovered in the discussion was that for years my wife had been moving toward a career, while I had been dreading losing more time with my family to a demanding job. Knowing I still had a weak job history and now an injury, we considered switching roles: I would take care of the family as my wife pursued her career.

Would it work for everyone? No, but it worked for us. My wife moved up the corporate ladder quickly, becoming a marketing manager for a major bookstore and media chain, while I found enjoyment in my new parental responsibilities as well as the time it gave me to take up writing again, a longtime hobby and now source of supplemental income. Plus, it gave me a chance to home school my daughter, fulfilling my longtime interest in education as a job option.

This was not the kind of success I would have dreamed up for me and my family. In fact, the idea of my wife being the main income provider is extremely contrary to how I grew up—and societal expectations. My career goals that I formed during high school are nowhere near what I'm doing now. Still, I can't imagine being happier with how things turned out. How many people can say that? I know our decision isn't for everyone, but it sure seems to be God's best for us.

I guess that's the true lesson for me behind my family's success. God had a plan specifically for us. And I believe He has a specific plan for you and your life. You may be surprised where the road to success will lead, but you will never get there giving up.

ACTION STEP

WE CAN'T LIVE IN A CONSTANT STATE OF INTROSPECTION, BUT SOMETIMES WE NEED TO STEP BACK FROM OUR OWN LIFE TO SEE HOW WE'RE DOING AND IF WE'RE ON COURSE.

Take a few minutes to do the following simple self-assessment:

NOT FULFILLED AT ALL------------------------------------ HIGHLY FULFILLED
AT WORK

NOT FULFILLED AT ALL------------------------------------ HIGHLY FULFILLED
IN FRIENDSHIPS

NOT FULFILLED AT ALL------------------------------------ HIGHLY FULFILLED
IN FAMILY LIFE

NOT FULFILLED AT ALL------------------------------------ HIGHLY FULFILLED
AT CHURCH

NOT FULFILLED AT ALL------------------------------------ HIGHLY FULFILLED
RELATIONSHIP WITH GOD

What are strength areas for you? What areas do you need to work on?

PRAYER

Dear Heavenly Father, I pray that today You would show me if I'm off track, and show me how to get where I need to be with You. Lord, thank You for Your guidance and love.

SPIRITUAL WARFARE

OUR BIGGEST BATTLES IN LIFE ARE IN THE SPIRITUAL REALM.

He who would fight the devil with his own weapons,
must not wonder if he finds him an overmatch.

ROBERT SOUTH

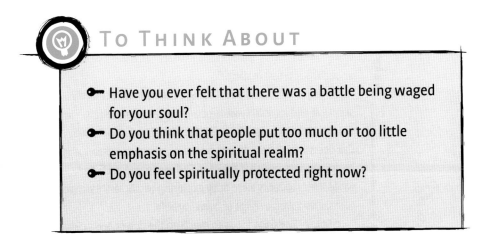

To Think About

- Have you ever felt that there was a battle being waged for your soul?
- Do you think that people put too much or too little emphasis on the spiritual realm?
- Do you feel spiritually protected right now?

LESSON FOR LIFE

PROMISES

PROMISES

God will—

Enable you to overcome
1 John 4:4

Enable you to stand
Ephesians 6:13

Deliver you from evil
2 Timothy 4:18

Protect you
James 4:7

Stand Strong

BIBLE STUDY PASSAGE: EPHESIANS 6:10-18

Jesus has the power of God, by which he has given us everything we need to live and to serve God. We have these things because we know him. Jesus called us by his glory and goodness.

2 PETER 1:3

C.S. Lewis, in his classic little book *The Screwtape Letters*, said: "There are two equal and opposite errors into which our race can fall about the devils. One is to disbelieve in their existence. The other is to believe, and to feel an excessive and unhealthy interest in them."

We live in a paradoxical culture that is both incredibly skeptical and incredibly wide open to any and all beliefs. In the classic book from 1965, *The Secular City*, author Harvey Cox described the conditions on many college campuses where professors lectured that belief in God was passé and dead, while their students were busy exploring witchcraft, earth religions, and a whole range of "new" beliefs.

Some Christians focus so much on the power and activity

of Satan that they live in a constant state of fear and uncertainty—or blame outside forces for all their shortcomings. Other Christians are so quick to explain away the supernatural that they live their lives with little or no reliance on God—and little spiritual power to really make a difference in the world.

When caring for your soul, it is good to remember—

- *The spiritual world—with both good and evil forces—is part of reality (Ephesians 6:12).*
- *Satan is intent on shipwrecking your faith—both through obvious attacks (1 Peter 5:8) and subtle temptations (2 Corinthians 11:14).*
- *We must put on the "armor" of God to withstand Satan's attacks, including faith, righteousness, truth, prayer, the Word of God, and salvation (Ephesians 6:14-18).*
- *We need not live in fear, for the grandest truth of all is that "God's Spirit, who is in you, is greater than the devil, who is in the world" (1 John 4:4).*

Be aware. Be alert. Humbly trust the Lord. Be bold with the confidence of loving and serving a mighty God!

We do live in the world, but we do not fight in the same way the world fights.

2 Corinthians 10:3

REAL LIFE

Nightmare

DON HALL AS TOLD TO NANETTE THORSEN-SNIPES

"Mom!" I shouted from my downstairs bedroom. Night had blanketed my shoulders and covered my face. I'd begun the night dreaming innocent dreams, but somehow they turned ugly. Evil. I knew my mom was asleep, but I was terrified. My whole body trembled at what my mind had weaved. In my nightmare, my father, who'd been dead several months, called me on the phone.

"Come down here," he said. In the dream, I knew what he meant—to hell. The dreams had gotten persistently worse and some involved what looked like demons.

I was only fifteen when he committed suicide, and though I didn't cry outwardly, I bawled on the inside. My parents had been divorced for years, and I rarely saw him. Now, I would never get to know him.

I took the stairs two at a time and ran until I stood at her bedroom door. "Mom!"

"What is it?" she asked sleepily.

I told her about my dream and how other dreams had been troubling me. She got out of bed and held me like a small child even though I was over six feet tall. My hands shook.

"Don't go back downstairs," she said. "Just stay up here with us."

I pulled away from her. I was all right. I could go back downstairs. I was a big boy now, and I was tough. In my bed again, I hugged my pillow close. Finally, I felt the sweet relief of sleep, but soon the nightmare crept in again. There was such evil in it. I knew God. I had even been baptized, but I'd turned away from Him thinking I could be a man—drinking and having fun.

From my bedroom, I screamed for Mom again.

In a moment, I heard her feet hit the floor. She raced down the stairs. "Please, Donnie," she said, "come upstairs." I refused.

She held her Bible close to her. "Let me read the Bible to you. It'll comfort you, son."

"No, I'm all right. I don't need God." I sat on the edge of my bed and felt tears snaking down my face.

"If you won't read God's Word, Donnie, please leave it on the nightstand," she said. "If you have another dream, just place your hand on the Bible."

She turned to leave, but must've had second thoughts. She came back and picked up the Bible and read 1 John 4:4. "God's Spirit, who is in you, is greater than the devil, who is in the world."

When the nightmare started again, I touched the Bible for reassurance. In time, the awful dreams began to vanish. Through the power of God's Word that my mother spoke and by just touching the Word, I found God's peace.

I am now a husband, a father, and a believer in Jesus Christ, and His peace makes my dreams sweet.

ACTION STEP

MEMORIZE SEVERAL SCRIPTURES THAT YOU CAN USE WHEN YOU FACE TEMP-
TATION OR FEEL THAT YOUR SPIRITUAL LIFE IS UNDER ATTACK. HERE ARE
FOUR THAT WOULD BE A GREAT START:

1. "The only temptation that has come to you is that which everyone has. But you can trust God, who will not permit you to be tempted more than you can stand. But when you are tempted, he will also give you a way to escape so that you will be able to stand it" (1 Corinthians 10:13).

2. "Also, the Spirit helps us with our weakness. We do not know how to pray as we should. But the Spirit himself speaks to God for us, even begs God for us with deep feelings that words cannot explain" (Romans 8:26).

3. "There is therefore now no condemnation to those who are in Christ Jesus, who do not walk according to the flesh, but according to the Spirit" (Romans 8:1 NKJV).

4. "So give yourselves completely to God. Stand against the devil, and the devil will run from you. Come near to God, and God will come near to you. You sinners, clean sin out of your lives. You who are trying to follow God and the world at the same time, make your thinking pure" (James 4:7-8).

PRAYER

Heavenly Father, with You inside me and beside me, I will not live life in fear. Thank You for giving me spiritual strength and boldness.

TRUSTING GOD

WHETHER TIMES ARE TOUGH OR EASY, FIRM BELIEF IN A GOOD AND LOVING GOD IS THE ONLY ROAD TO VIBRANT LIVING.

When you have nothing left but God, then for the first time you become aware that God is enough.

MAUDE ROYDEN

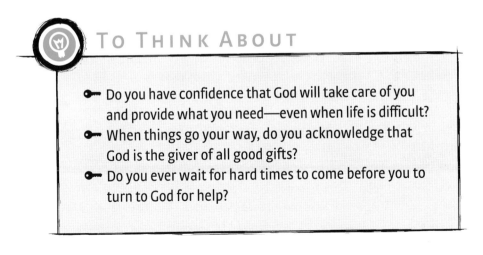

TO THINK ABOUT

- Do you have confidence that God will take care of you and provide what you need—even when life is difficult?
- When things go your way, do you acknowledge that God is the giver of all good gifts?
- Do you ever wait for hard times to come before you to turn to God for help?

LESSON FOR LIFE

PROMISES

God will—

Give you peace
Isaiah 26:3

Take care of you
Nahum 1:7

Be with you
Psalm 23:4

Guide your steps
Proverbs 3:5-6

Hear your prayers
Psalm 18:6

Give you refuge
Isaiah 4:5-6

Daily Dependence

BIBLE STUDY PASSAGE: PSALM 40:3-5

Trust the Lord with all your heart, and don't depend on your own understanding. Remember the Lord in all you do, and he will give you success.

PROVERBS 3:5-6

We rightfully teach our children—and attempt to live our own lives—by the credos of responsibility, self-control, and mature self-reliance.

And yes, being responsible is a very good thing. But when our attitude reaches the point where we trust more in ourselves than in God, twin temptations, both that lead to spiritual shipwreck, suddenly confront us.

One temptation is pride, an unhealthy arrogance that slips (or roars) into our thinking when things are going great in our lives. We become convinced that we are in control of our own world.

The second temptation, despair, works itself into our hearts when we face the inevitable difficulties and setbacks of life that are outside of our control—illness, a difficult relationship, an economic downturn.

Daily trusting in God—acknowledging that He is the one source of all good gifts and success and the only safe refuge when life is difficult—steers us from the twin dangers of pride and despair.

Jesus once pointed to a little child and said, "I tell you the truth, you must change and become like little children. Otherwise, you will never enter the kingdom of heaven. The greatest person in the kingdom of heaven is the one who makes himself humble like this child" (Matthew 18:3-4). A child's humility is one of trust—it pleases God when we trust Him as a child trusts and depends on his father.

James points out that trials test and prove our faith (James 1:1-3), but we don't have to wait for challenging moments to begin trusting God with our entire life. The good news is that with complete and total trust in Him, He directs our steps in the most fulfilling paths for our lives.

We rejoice in him,
because we trust his
holy name.
Psalm 33:21

REAL LIFE

Still Skiing

KENT PALMER AS TOLD TO GLENDA PALMER

After I graduated from high school in southern California, I moved to Lake Tahoe to work at the ski resort during the winter. Later, when I was twenty-two, I fulfilled another dream—a helicopter ski trip with my cousin Todd to Banff, British Columbia. The pilot dropped us off at the top of the mountain and we skied down the pristine slopes uncluttered by other skiers and chair lifts. As I carved turns in the powdery snow, I felt a new closeness to God.

But after that trip, my back began to hurt. I usually didn't worry about sore muscles or aching bones because little injuries were common to me, something to shrug off. I worked in construction and stayed active in sports. But this pain was different. Finally, I told my mom, "My back hurts so bad, I can't surf." So she called for a doctor's appointment. Even being my mom, though, she wasn't particularly concerned.

The doctor performed some tests, then phoned me to say he was admitting me to the hospital immediately for surgery. "It looks like a large tumor," he said. "It may be malignant."

Dad, Mom, and my brother, Scott, met the doctors at the hospital. Despite the seriousness of the situation, my brother and I joked around like always. That helped. The morning of the operation, when the surgeon explained the procedure to us, he asked if I had any questions. I said, "Yeah, what's for lunch?"

But, deep inside, I felt helpless. I was a Christian who went to church and prayed, but I never cried out to God like I did that night alone in the hospital before the surgery. *Lord Jesus, please help me.*

It didn't turn out the way we hoped. The doctor came into my room and said, "It was a malignant nine-pound tumor attached to the aorta artery. I couldn't remove it all because you started to hemorrhage." My morphine drip couldn't touch the pain of hearing those words. I didn't know why God would allow this to happen to me.

I fought back by claiming God's promise in Jeremiah 29:11: "'I know what I am planning for you,' says the Lord. 'I have good plans for you, not plans to hurt you. I will give you hope and a good future.'" People prayed as I underwent chemotherapy and a second major surgery to remove the rest of the tumor from the aorta. I prayed, too, *I trust You, Lord, even if Your answer is no.* Between hospitalizations, I studied and earned a real estate license. I kept my eyes on the future, not on fear or death, but on hope and life.

God answered our prayers with a yes. Sixteen years later, I'm a busy mortgage consultant, married to a great wife, Angie, with a fourteen-year-old daughter, Cassie. We are a church-going, fun-loving family that likes to travel, fish, surf, and snowboard. And each day, in some way, I feel that thankfulness I knew skiing the mountains of Banff.

ACTION STEP

READ THROUGH HEBREWS 11 IN YOUR NEW TESTAMENT, WHICH PROVIDES A LIST OF OLD TESTAMENT CHARACTERS WHO COMPLETELY TRUSTED GOD— AGAINST ALL ODDS. NOW THINK OF THE TWO OR THREE MOST DIFFICULT MOMENTS IN THE LAST FEW YEARS OF YOUR LIFE. DID YOU FACE THOSE TIMES WITH FAITH IN GOD? IF NOT, HOW WOULD FAITH HAVE MADE A POSITIVE DIFFERENCE?

PRAYER

Dear God, I give to You every difficulty, fear, and uncertainty—along with every success and good thing—and trust You to provide the strength and grace, the perspective and poise I need to trust You in all the situations of my life.

FATHERHOOD

BEING A GREAT DADDY IS PERHAPS THE MOST CHALLENGING AND REWARDING UNDERTAKING FOR ANY MAN.

What God is to the world, parents are to children.

PHILO

TO THINK ABOUT

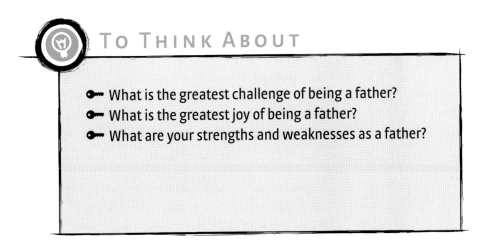

- What is the greatest challenge of being a father?
- What is the greatest joy of being a father?
- What are your strengths and weaknesses as a father?

LESSON FOR LIFE

PROMISES

God will—

Bless your
parenting efforts
Proverbs 22:6

Protect the fatherless
Jeremiah 49:11

Bless your children
Psalm 112:2

Show you how to teach
your children
Psalm 78:5-6

A Short Course on Fatherhood

BIBLE STUDY PASSAGE: 1 CORINTHIANS 4:14-16

So the son left and went to his father. While the son was still a long way off, his father saw him and felt sorry for his son. So the father ran to him and hugged and kissed him.

LUKE 15:20

If you are a father, you have one of the most respected and demanding titles ever given to man. It isn't always easy, but is there any endeavor more rewarding?

You may have everything under control in your home—or you may feel as though you are swimming upstream—but all fathers can benefit from the following principles:

- *Give kids time. We live in a prosperous world that equates material blessings with love. That's not how kids see it. Kids spell "love" with four letters: T-I-M-E.*
- *Be quick to listen (James 1:19). Yes, kids need your wisdom and thoughts on a variety of topics, but particularly as they enter adolescence, they need someone who will ask a lot of questions and listen. Listening can be much harder than*

talking—but you'll be amazed how smart it makes you!
- *Be slow to anger (James 1:19). The fruit of the Spirit includes love, peace, patience, and self-control (Galatians 5:22-23). Paul counsels fathers not to "exasperate your children" (Ephesians 6:4) through harshness.*
- *Provide loving discipline (Proverbs 13:24). When we don't hold our children accountable for their words and actions, we aren't doing them any favors or showing more love. In fact, the writer of Hebrews says that the father who doesn't discipline his son lacks love (Hebrews 12:5-8). Children need a firm, gentle, consistent presence in their lives.*
- *Dedicate your children to God. This is more than a special ceremony at church when our children are babies. We must daily commit them to God through prayer in the good times and the bad times. What better gift can you give your child than to tell them, "I pray for you every day"?*

A loving father is crucial to the development of a child's soul. Be encouraged as you embrace the honor and responsibility of being a father!

Fathers, do not make your children angry, but raise them with the training and teaching of the Lord.
Ephesians 6:4

REAL LIFE

My Rebel

JIM SNIPES AS TOLD TO NANETTE THORSEN-SNIPES

When my oldest two stepchildren were young, I gave them chores. Not only did they do the usual daily chores, they also helped me in our garden.

David, ten, and seven-year-old Donnie helped me plant squash, pole beans, cucumbers, and tomatoes in a sunny spot beside our house. Both boys helped put the seeds into the soil. Later, when the time came to weed the garden, Donnie balked.

"My feet hurt," he'd say, but I urged him on. Later, he would whine again, "My leg hurts, I can't do it." I joked with him, but insisted he finish what he had started.

Donnie soon became a teen. In time, he got into trouble with drinking and staying out late.

At the supper table one night, I questioned him about his late-night activities. "As long as you live in this house," I reminded him, "you are answerable to me."

Donnie erupted in anger. "You can't tell me what to do. You're not my father! I'll do anything I want!"

I leapt from my seat and grabbed the front of his T-shirt, yanking him from the chair. I shoved him hard against the wall. We stood face-to-face, so close I could smell his breath. I began yelling, "You will do what I say! You got that?"

When I finished, Donnie said something under his breath and slammed out the back door.

Immediately, I called out to God. I loved my son. I didn't want to alienate him, yet that was exactly what I was doing. I could feel the Holy Spirit piercing my heart, convicting me.

I went downstairs and read my Bible. Then I pulled up my office chair and knelt beside it. Bowing my head, I prayed for forgiveness.

A few months later, Donnie totaled his small car. Again, he reminded me I was not his father and he could do anything he wanted. Eventually, he landed in jail for taking an unloaded gun into a bar.

I figured time in the county jail was good for him. And it was. It brought Donnie back to his senses and to a new relationship with God. He later met and married a wonderful girl named Jennifer, and they now have two children.

A year ago, my two oldest boys and their families came to visit for Father's Day. At ages thirty-eight and thirty-five, they made handsome men, and I was proud of them. I motioned for them to meet me outside on the deck.

I sat on the porch swing while they sat across from me. "You boys know how much I love you, don't you?"

Each of them nodded.

"I know I'm not your father, and I never will be. But would it be possible for you to call me Dad?" I swallowed hard, not knowing where I stood with them.

"No problem, Dad," said David.

Just as quickly, Donnie grinned and said, "Sure, Dad."

I felt as though my Father had just reached down from heaven and blessed me. It hadn't always been easy to be a father; there were certainly moments of struggle. But hearing the word "Dad" made the entire journey blessed and wonderful.

ACTION STEP

WHEN WAS THE LAST TIME YOU TOOK YOUR KID OUT ON A "DATE"? NO AGENDA. NO RUSH. JUST TIME. MAKE PLANS TODAY! YOU—AND YOUR CHILD—WILL BE GLAD YOU DID.

PRAYER

Thank You, Heavenly Father, that You have blessed me with children. Help me to teach them what a loving God You are by the way I love them.

SHARING GOD'S LOVE

OUT OF GRATITUDE FOR WHAT GOD HAS DONE FOR US, WE ARE TO SHARE HIS LOVE AND FORGIVENESS WITH OTHERS.

Our love to God is measured by our everyday fellowship with others and the love it displays.

ANDREW MURRAY

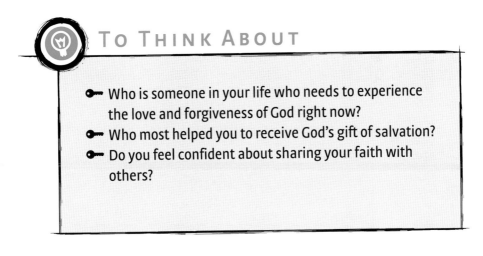

TO THINK ABOUT

- Who is someone in your life who needs to experience the love and forgiveness of God right now?
- Who most helped you to receive God's gift of salvation?
- Do you feel confident about sharing your faith with others?

LESSON FOR LIFE

PROMISES

God will—

Reveal himself in our
love for each other
John 13:35

See our love for Him in
the way we treat
each other
John 21:15-17

Reward displays of love
Hebrews 6:10

Always love us
Romans 8:39

Love Each Other

BIBLE STUDY PASSAGE: 1 JOHN 2:7-10

*All people will know that you are my followers if you love
each other.*

JOHN 13:35

When Peter wrote to a small group of Christians who were
persecuted and made fun of for being Christians, he said:
"Always be ready to answer everyone who asks you to explain
about the hope you have" (1 Peter 3:15).

That means that all of us should be prepared to tell others
how we know God is real and has made us into a new person
through Jesus Christ. Have you ever thought through what you
would say to someone who wants to have a personal relationship with God? Do you have a couple of Bible verses memo-
rized that you could share with them? Would you be ready to
pray with them?

But just as important as having words to say is the way we
live our lives. Many people have quit going to church because
of the bad attitudes and activities of those who call themselves
Christians. Jesus tells his disciples that the easiest way people

will know that they have a real and powerful relationship with God is by how they love one another.

One of the greatest and most powerful descriptions of love is found in 1 Corinthians 13, where Paul says: "Love is patient and kind. Love is not jealous, it does not brag, and it is not proud. Love is not rude, is not selfish, and does not get upset with others. Love does not count up wrongs that have been done" (vv. 4-5).

How about you? Do you show love to your family through your words and your actions? To your friends and coworkers? Are you helping the people in your life draw closer to God?

Hatred stirs up trouble, but love forgives all wrongs.
Proverbs 10:12

REAL LIFE

Am I My Brother's Keeper?

DAVID KILBY AS TOLD TO KAREN KILBY

Someone once asked me, "What will you do about your brother after your dad dies?" My first thought was, *Am I my brother's keeper?*

"He's a big boy, he can take care of himself," I'd quickly retorted. After all, Doug was not a child—he was a grown man, despite all of his childish escapades. He was thirty-five. High time he learned to be responsible.

But shortly after the tragic deaths of our father and mother, the question was raised once again—what would happen with Doug? I had just moved my family from Florida to Michigan, leaving Doug behind. Now he was alone and wanted to be close to us. How could we refuse?

Doug found a room at the local hotel and seemed to be content just to be near us. He worked at odd jobs to keep a roof over his head and a supply of beer in the refrigerator, happy to be included in our family activities.

When we moved back to Florida three years later, Doug followed. Doug was not the easiest person to be around, despite his droll sense of humor. He had a habit of telling whoppers to build up his self-esteem and things could get out of hand when he had too much to drink. A little bit of Doug went a long way.

But God gave me patience, and I came to a major realization one day. Once again the question, *Am I my brother's keeper?* ran through my mind as I realized that Doug needed help to stop drinking.

Wanting to please me, Doug agreed to participate in a rehabilitation program, not thinking there would be any real benefit. There he met Martha. Martha thought Doug was the funniest man she had ever met. Laughter was therapy for her, and she could not get enough of Doug's humor. A year later, they were married.

As they settled into their marriage, I felt that David needed a chance to prove himself, so I decided to give him a job with my company. Wearing a suit and carrying a briefcase made Doug look like a new man. I didn't realize a change was taking place inside of Doug as well. Now that Doug felt worthy of being accepted, he wanted to go to church with us—another chance to wear a suit and tie. Sunday after Sunday, Doug and Martha would dress their best and join us in church. Week after week, Doug heard about God's unconditional love.

Shortly before Doug became deathly ill from diabetes, he wrote me a letter. "I used to think Christians were nothing but a bunch of hypocrites and vowed I would never become one," he wrote. "Over the years I have scrutinized your life and have come to realize you are not. I am proud to say my brother is a Christian and thankful to say that I am, too."

ACTION STEP

ON A NOTECARD, WRITE DOWN THE NAME OF FIVE PEOPLE IN YOUR LIFE WHO NEED TO EXPERIENCE THE LOVE AND FORGIVENESS OF GOD. COMMIT YOUR-SELF TO PRAY FOR THEM BY NAME EACH DAY. AS YOU PRAY FOR THEM, ASK GOD TO GIVE YOU THE CONFIDENCE AND WISDOM TO TALK WITH THEM AT THE RIGHT TIME. ASK HIM TO PROVIDE A PERFECT OPPORTUNITY.

PRAYER

Father God, I realize today that people really need You. Please use me to direct them toward You.

SEXUAL PURITY

A KEY BATTLE FOR YOUR SOUL IS IN THE AREA OF SEXUAL PURITY.

The reason why many fail in battle is because they wait until the hour of battle. The reason why others succeed is because they have gained their victory on their knees long before the battle came. Anticipate your battles; fight them on your knees before temptation comes, and you will always have victory.

R.A. TORREY

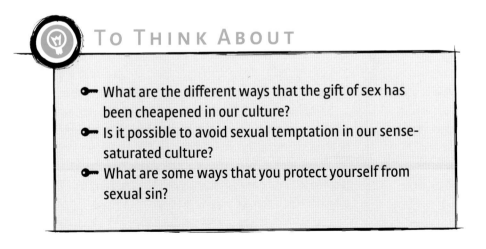

TO THINK ABOUT

- What are the different ways that the gift of sex has been cheapened in our culture?
- Is it possible to avoid sexual temptation in our sense-saturated culture?
- What are some ways that you protect yourself from sexual sin?

LESSON FOR LIFE

PROMISES:

God will—

Give you healthy, enjoyable relationships
Song of Songs 7:6

Forgive and refresh you
Acts 3:19

Justify you apart from your record of perfection or imperfection
Acts 13:38-39

Renew you and make you like Christ
Colossians 3:10

Honor God with Your Body

BIBLE STUDY PASSAGE: 1 THESSALONIANS 4:1-8

Keep on working to complete your salvation with fear and trembling, because God is working in you to help you want to do and be able to do what pleases him.

PHILIPPIANS 2:12-13

Perhaps the greatest temptation that is known to man has been around for centuries: lust.

The great biblical figure Joseph had his boss's wife persistently attempt to seduce him. Understanding the consequences to his soul, he fled, serving as a great role model of purity (Genesis 39:7-12). He was falsely accused and punished—but God took care of him and rewarded him for his faithfulness.

King David did not fare quite so well in his battle with lust. When he saw a beautiful woman sunbathing on a nearby roof, he allowed temptation to turn into active pursuit. He became an adulterer—and to cover up his sin, a murderer. Even though forgiven by God, he and all those around him, including his kingdom, paid a horrible price for his sin.

So, how do we stay pure in mind and body an X-rated world?

- Avoid temptation when possible. Not all things that stimulate impure thoughts can be avoided, but there are people, places, and situations we can steer clear of. When possible, starve the source (Ephesians 5:3, Matthew 5:29).
- Recognize sex as a marvelous gift from God to be honored in marriage (Hebrews 13:4). There is nothing shameful or dirty about the human body and our sexuality. God created us this way. We would do better not to diminish our sexuality, but to thank God for His plans for our lives.
- Foster positive relationships and accountability (2 Timothy 2:22, James 5:16). If you are married, make yours the most loving, dynamic, affectionate marriage in the world. No excuses. You're not that tired. Love your wife passionately. If you are single, make sure you avail yourself of numerous opportunities to be around others in healthy and wholesome activities.
- Realize that God provides the strength to overcome temptation: "And now he can help those who are tempted, because he himself suffered and was tempted" (Hebrews 2:18).

More men are spiritually shipwrecked by sexual sin than perhaps any other temptation. Don't let Satan rob you of God's blessing for living with purity.

So run away from sexual sin. Every other sin people do is outside their bodies, but those who sin sexually sin against their own bodies.
1 Corinthians 6:18

49

 ## REAL LIFE

Easy Lover

JAY COOKINGHAM

Sam's* gaze lingered longer than it should have on the curvy figure that passed us.   When I reminded him of his marital status, Sam said, "Hey, just because I'm on a diet doesn't mean I can't look at the menu."

I was seventeen, and he was the church youth leader I admired.   Equating women with menu choices was not an observation a young man already struggling with lust needed to hear.   My view of the opposite sex blurred further, and consequently, my battle to stay pure before marriage took a huge hit.   It was about to take a greater one.

One day I discovered a stash of pornographic material my father had hidden in the attic.   Before long, porn had become my easy lover, a secret rendezvous with fantasy and excitement.   I convinced myself that I could manage it, that I was in control.   What I didn't see was that every liaison with pornography exacted a toll on my values and my resolve.

Soon, my lust-filled desires spilled over to my romantic encounters.   The "heat of the moment" decisions that followed allowed a precious gift to be wasted.   Sadly, even losing my virginity didn't convince me of the downward spiral I was in.

It took a broken-off marriage engagement to finally alert me that my life needed changing.   Heartbroken and ashamed of my behavior, I began pouring out my pain to God.

Surrendering my easy-lover lifestyle to Him was the only way to be free. I knew that, but relinquishing that control was a leap of faith for me. It was a battle—porn was a jealous lover, and there were times I didn't want to let go either.

However, as I gave God first-place status in my love life, my faith grew bolder. To hold me accountable, I asked mature men to check in on my activities. While I prayed for a renewed mind, I also changed my "viewing" habits. The scripture Job 31:1, "I made an agreement with my eyes not to look with desire at a girl," was a great aid in enabling me to see women as His precious daughters, not entrées on some menu. While it was true that I was no longer a virgin, with God's help I could still win the war for my purity.

What followed was a time of cleansing, and out of that season of surrender came a real miracle. Not only did I find victory in my struggle, I met and married the love of my life, my wife, Christine. This pure God-centered relationship was a gift more valuable than I ever imagined. Together we dealt with my issues of the past, while learning how to be deeply intimate with each other. My marriage is now an ongoing covenant romance of twenty-two years, making my former easy lover a distant memory.

ACTION STEP

Is there a source of temptation in your life that needs to be starved? Certain TV channels or websites? A flirtatious relationship that you have not really avoided? A negative dynamic in your marriage? Determine one thing you can change today and go for it!

PRAYER

O God, You created us to live life fully, with joy and pleasure. Help me to obey Your Word and follow Your direction so that I can live with purity and purpose.

FACING AN UNCERTAIN FUTURE

THOUGH WE DON'T KNOW WHAT TOMORROW HOLDS, WE CAN TRUST GOD TO SEE US THROUGH.

We do not understand the intricate pattern of the stars in their courses, but we know that He who created them does, and that just as surely as He guides them, He is charting a safe course for us.

BILLY GRAHAM

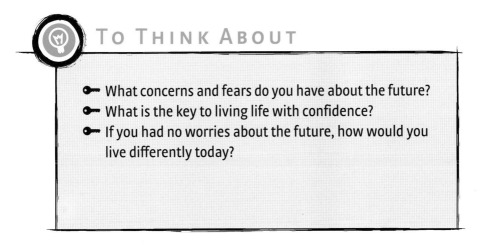

TO THINK ABOUT

- What concerns and fears do you have about the future?
- What is the key to living life with confidence?
- If you had no worries about the future, how would you live differently today?

LESSON FOR LIFE

PROMISES:

God will—

Stay by your side
in danger
Joshua 1:9

Make you strong
and wise
Job 9:4

Turn even tragedy into
good for you
Romans 8:28

Make you strong
Joshua 1:5

If God Is for Us

BIBLE STUDY PASSAGE: NUMBERS 13

The Lord says, "Whoever loves me, I will save.   I will protect those who know me.   They will call to me, and I will answer them.   I will be with them in trouble; I will rescue them and honor them.   I will give them a long, full life, and they will see how I can save."

PSALM 91:14-16

The investor's credo tells us that past performance is the best predictor, but not a guarantee, of future results.   A company or an index or a sports team can perform magnificently for years—but tomorrow is still another day.

Moses led the children of Israel out of captivity in Egypt, through the wilderness, and to the edge of the Promised Land (Numbers 13:1).   He passed the responsibility of leadership to Joshua, who sent out twelve spies in preparation for crossing the Jordan River.   Ten of the spies returned with tales of giants and mighty warriors who would never allow them to enter what was supposed to be their new home; two of the spies returned with tales of a land of milk and honey—ripe for the taking (Numbers 13:27-33).

Maybe all twelve spies were right, but Caleb, who was ready to cross the river that day, understood the only hope the children of Israel had for the future: "If the Lord is pleased with us, he will lead us into that land and give us that fertile land" (Numbers 14:8).

Though the future is unpredictable and there are few guarantees, we can cling to the promise that God is "the same yesterday, today, and forever" (Hebrews 13:8) and that His "faithfulness endures to all generations" (Psalm 119:90 NKJV).

It's that promise that allowed a young shepherd boy named David to defeat a giant (1 Samuel 17:37, 49), and then declare as an old man who had survived and conquered in the midst of many battles: "Horses can't bring victory; they can't save by their strength. But the Lord looks after those who fear him, those who put their hope in his love" (Psalm 33:17-18).

Do you have challenges ahead? Undoubtedly! But when you love and walk with the Creator of the universe, you have nothing to fear.

So don't worry, because I am with you. Don't be afraid, because I am your God. I will make you strong and will help you; I will support you with my right hand that saves you.
Isaiah 41:10

 REAL LIFE

Lesson from Desert Storm

DR. DANNY SMITH AS TOLD TO KAYLEEN J. REUSSER

A succession of deafening explosions ripped through the night, awakening me from a fitful sleep. Immediately, I put on my gas mask and bolted from the cot to join other personnel at the barracks windows.

Black smoke and flying debris obliterated our view of the war-torn Kuwaiti desert. The cacophony of noise sounded different from the other times when we had been fired at by one of Saddam Hussein's low-flying Soviet Scud missiles. Later we learned that a seventeen-foot Allied rocket, the Patriot, had streaked through the sky, breaking the sound barrier and destroying an incoming Scud in a fiery collision.

It was history's first wartime intercept of a ballistic missile. A television crew on the roof of a nearby building caught the event on film so that millions of American viewers could watch it.

I was platoon commander of the Army National Guard medical unit stationed out of Iowa City, Iowa. Our unit had been deployed to Kuwait in January 1991 as part of a massive military buildup by the United States to combat Saddam Hussein's invasion of Kuwait. Our mission was to perform advance trauma life support, stabilize the wounded, and send them back to the MASH unit or field hospital in the rear.

We hadn't been there long when medical intelligence told us that due to an increase in air strikes, we should expect 500 to 1,000 casualties a day.

As a Christian, I often sought comfort and help in dealing with the tragedies of war from Psalm 91. The words, written thousands of years ago, seemed to fit our twentieth-century situation and give me assurance that God was in control.

The next day, I ordered the entire platoon to assemble. "No one knows when this thing will end or if any of us will walk away from it," I told them. "I've been scared and I think most of you have been too. But I believe Someone greater than Saddam is watching over us. God, our Creator, loves us and is able to protect us." Then I read Psalm 91.

Afterward, several people thanked me for reading the scripture. During the next few days, I noticed soldiers reading the New Testaments issued to them.

It wasn't until two days later, when 160 of us were sent up to the front line to support the Third Artillery Division from Seventh Corps out of Europe, that I saw how powerful God's Word could be. While the number of casualties in our unit increased, they were mostly minor shrapnel injuries. We never did have the hundreds of battle-related casualties that medical intelligence had predicted. When the Allied forces called a truce with Saddam, we praised God that our entire unit had escaped with little injury. A few weeks later, our platoon returned safely to the States.

With God's protection and help through His Word, we made it. I never stop praying for soldiers in harm's way today that they, too, can know the peace of God, even in the midst of an uncertain future.

ACTION STEP

ONE OF THE GREAT SPIRITUAL DISCIPLINES THAT HAS BEEN ALL BUT LOST IN OUR MODERN WORLD OF INSTANT INFORMATION IS THE ART OF MEMORIZATION. DAVID TELLS US "YOUR WORD I HAVE HIDDEN IN MY HEART, THAT I MIGHT NOT SIN AGAINST YOU" (PSALM 119:11 NKJV) AND "HOW I LOVE YOUR TEACHINGS! I THINK ABOUT THEM ALL DAY LONG" (PSALM 119:97). READ THE FOLLOWING BIBLE VERSES AND SELECT AT LEAST ONE TO MEMORIZE AND RECALL AS YOU FACE UNCERTAINTIES IN LIFE:

- "My grace is enough for you. When you are weak, my power is made perfect in you." (2 Corinthians 12:9)
- "The everlasting God is your place of safety, and his arms will hold you up forever." (Deuteronomy 33:27)
- "Jesus said, 'Don't let your hearts be troubled. Trust in God, and trust in me.'" (John 14:1)
- "The Lord God is my strength. He makes me like a deer that does not stumble so I can walk on the steep mountains." (Habakkuk 3:19)
- "God did not give us a spirit that makes us afraid but a spirit of power and love and self-control." (2 Timothy 1:7)

PRAYER

Lord God, I need Your strength to face the challenges in my life. I commit myself and my future to You today.

THE JOY OF WORK

GOD CREATED US TO BE PRODUCTIVE AND RESPONSIBLE.

I've met a few people in my time who were enthusiastic about hard work.   And it was just my luck that all of them happened to be men I was working for at the time.

BILL GOLD

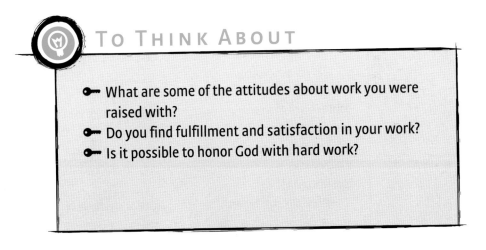

TO THINK ABOUT

- ❧ What are some of the attitudes about work you were raised with?
- ❧ Do you find fulfillment and satisfaction in your work?
- ❧ Is it possible to honor God with hard work?

LESSON FOR LIFE

PROMISES

God will—

Bless your hard work
Proverbs 10:4
Proverbs 12:11

Guide you
Psalm 48:14

Multiply your talents
Matthew 25:21

Help you
Psalm 33:20

The Daily Grind

BIBLE STUDY PASSAGE: GENESIS 3:16-24

Wealth gained by dishonesty will be diminished, but he who gathers by labor will increase.

PROVERBS 13:11 NKJV

God created us to be productive and have fulfilling work—"The Lord God put the man in the garden of Eden to care for it and work it" (Genesis 2:15). The reason that so many of us don't find work satisfying is explained in the same ancient passage—"So I will put a curse on the ground, and you will have to work very hard for your food. In pain you will eat its food all the days of your life" (Genesis 3:17).

No wonder work creates feelings of ambiguity: It is ordained of God and necessary for sustaining house and home, but somehow in the process of sin entering the world, work becomes at times toilsome and unproductive.

Since you will probably spend more time and energy in work than any other area of your life, you'd better come to peace with this essential part of life.

• *Work with thankfulness: "Everything you do or say should be done to obey Jesus your Lord. And in all you do, give thanks to*

God the Father through Jesus" (Colossians 3:17). Too many individuals gripe and complain about work. But consider the person
who is unemployed or underemployed. They can tell you that it's
much harder not to work than to work. Be thankful!

- *Work with your whole heart:* "In all the work you are doing, work
the best you can. Work as if you were doing it for the Lord, not
for people" (Colossians 3:23). We lose self-respect and the respect
of others when we do a shoddy job at work. Jesus tells us: "You
should be a light for other people. Live so that they will see the
good things you do and will praise your Father in heaven"
(Matthew 5:16).
- *Work in the areas of your gifts:* "We all have different gifts, each
of which came because of the grace God gave us" (see Romans
12:6-8). Seek career counseling. Today! And also consider that
your job may be a means of doing what you really want to—
spending time with family and ministering to others.
- *Work is not most important:* "Love the Lord your God with all
your heart, all your soul, and all your mind." This is the first and
most important command (Matthew 22:37-38). Yes, work is an
important part of who we are as men, but nothing surpasses the
importance of our souls.

Life is too short to hate or avoid work. Today is the day to
find—or create—fulfillment in all you do!

Whatever work you do,
do your best.
Ecclesiastes 9:10

REAL LIFE

You Da Man!

JIM SNIPES AS TOLD TO NANETTE THORSEN-SNIPES

While I wanted my stepson to go to college, I knew that with three other mouths to feed and mounting bills from my wife's arthritis, it would have to wait.

I was proud, however, as he walked down the aisle and accepted his high school diploma. I didn't know how he'd ever be able to get further than a waiter at a four-star restaurant. But he did.

Years later, I asked David how he became so successful. We had lived a hard life—beginning with my marrying his mother and taking on two young sons. Within three years, we were a family of six with the addition of a daughter and another son.

When Nan developed a ruptured disk and sciatica, she stopped work and went on long-term disability, leaving us with hospital bills and half our salary. When we got behind on the car payments, we even lost our cars.

We were short on prayer during those early years, but we raised the kids the best we could. We taught them responsibility and made them do chores. They bellyached, but they learned fortitude.

As they grew older, Nan began seeking God again. She found a church and went every Sunday, taking the kids with her.

Eventually, I caved and began to attend church, too. I guess the experiences of an early work ethic and church led David to the hospitality industry.

Unbelievably, David rose to the top, becoming the general manager of a prominent Atlanta hotel and was successful beyond imagination.

One day, he told me of an orientation he had for new employees. A housekeeper asked how he'd become general manager.

"My dad made sure I was responsible," he said. "He made us work hard at everything we did, and we were not allowed to quit."

At fourteen, he'd become the very best busboy in the hotel. Once he'd mastered that, he became the very best back waiter, making desserts and Caesar salads at tableside. The bottom line was that David always did the best he could.

Step by step, he moved up, achieving almost everything he set his mind to. From waiter to restaurant manager to marketing manager, nothing was impossible.

As David talked, I realized the more prominent his position became, the more he remembered the "little" guy, something I instilled in him from my renewed walk with Jesus.

I was thrilled to learn he remembered how Jesus loved others and put it into action. David said he attempted to eat lunch with the chef, talk with the doorman or fold linens with housekeeping, who sometimes greeted him with, "You da man!"

During the orientation, David said someone asked about his cufflinks.

"Those aren't your initials, are they?" the woman had asked.

David grinned. No, YDM weren't his initials. Employees from his former job had surprised him with the special cufflinks when he changed hotels.

"I knew I'd reached the pinnacle of my profession," he said, "when I left and my whole staff shouted, "You da man!"

ACTION STEP

WHAT IS ONE THING YOU CAN DO MORE OF AT WORK TO BE MORE PRODUCTIVE? MORE SALES CALLS? BETTER MEMOS? BETTER RELATIONSHIPS WITH PEERS OR CUSTOMERS? KEEP A SIMPLE LOG BESIDE YOU AND MONITOR THAT YOU DO MORE OF IT. LIKEWISE, WHAT IS ONE THING YOU DO AT WORK THAT RUINS PRODUCTIVITY? HOW CAN YOU DO LESS OF THIS?

PRAYER

Thank You, O God, for the opportunity to bless myself, my family, my church, and my world both through my job and what I receive materially from work.

OVERCOMING FEAR

THOUGH FEAR IS A NATURAL HUMAN RESPONSE,
WE CAN FACE ANYTHING LIFE THROWS OUR WAY
WITH CONFIDENCE THROUGH TRUST IN GOD.

If the Lord be with us, we have no cause of fear.
His eye is upon us, His arm over us, His ear open to our prayer,
His grace sufficient, His promise unchangeable.

JOHN NEWTON

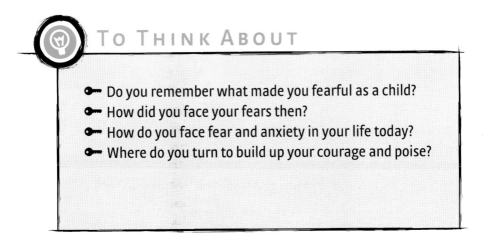

TO THINK ABOUT

- Do you remember what made you fearful as a child?
- How did you face your fears then?
- How do you face fear and anxiety in your life today?
- Where do you turn to build up your courage and poise?

LESSON FOR LIFE

PROMISES:

God will—

Protect you
from enemies
Psalm 18:3

Be with you
Isaiah 41:10

Preserve you
from calamity
2 Samuel 22:19

Give you what you need
to do His will
Hebrews 13:20

Help you in your work
Isaiah 26:12

Baby Steps

BIBLE STUDY PASSAGE: PHILIPPIANS 4:4-7

Jesus said, "Come." And Peter left the boat and walked on the water to Jesus.

MATTHEW 14:29

Nothing can rob you of joy, confidence, optimism, and opportunities more quickly than a spirit of fear—even if it's hard for us men to even admit to having fear!

Behavioral scientists have long debated whether the first emotion a baby experiences is love or fear. Because of the "startle reflex," many researchers believe it is the latter. So even if it doesn't feel macho to be afraid sometimes, realize you were born this way!

When faced with danger, the two foundational responses that appear to be "hard-wired" into the human psyche are fight and flight. So are you a fight or a flight person?

There are many sources of fear. Some are unreasonable (to everyone else but the persons experiencing them!), and are considered unhealthy phobias. But whatever the source—a sense of the unknown, the future, physical danger, spiritual warfare, financial crises, or reputation issues—fear is real and must be faced honestly.

One of the greatest promises of God is that we don't have to face our fears alone. He is always with us; never will He forsake us (Hebrews 13:5). In fact, when we truly experience His love, fear is cast away (1 John 4:18). Why? Love is what must be present in any relationship for trust to flourish. So remember, if you fear—

- *your past: God makes all things new (2 Corinthians 5:17);*
- *your future: God has promised you a future and a hope (Jeremiah 29:11);*
- *your enemies: God will protect and keep you (Deuteronomy 31:6);*
- *financial problems: God will provide for your every need (Philippians 4:19);*
- *death and dying: God has conquered the power of death and promises eternal life (Romans 8:1-2).*

Are you ready to walk boldly, with a new sense of confidence today? Take a few steps, even if they're baby steps, toward God and let Him handle all the anxieties that trouble you.

Be strong and brave. Don't be afraid of them and don't be frightened, because the Lord your God will go with you. He will not leave you or forget you.
Deuteronomy 31:6

REAL LIFE

Vaya Con Dios

TERRY HIGGINBOTHAM

"The biopsy results came back 'suspiciously benign,'" my doctor stated matter-of-factly.

"What does that mean?"

"It means we can't rule out cancer."

For the last three weeks, there had hardly been a moment that I wasn't thinking about my last doctor's consultation. I couldn't help it—I was scared.

Ever since Pastor Tim announced that our church was going to take the gospel outside our "Jerusalem," I longed to be part of the action—a team from our church would be going to Juarez, Mexico, to build houses with a group called Casas Por Christos. But the doctor's words were just another reason to doubt my ability to minister, another reason to be afraid of stepping out of my comfort zone.

I had been praying for an opportunity to step out in faith and serve my Lord. My wife, Colleen, and I had discussed it that very morning, and God had hit my heart with a lightening bolt. But in that moment of embracing our great and wise God and committing to go to Juarez, Satan began hammering at the fear in my heart—was it really a good idea to leave the country when I might have a life-threatening illness?

Some would call me foolish, but I decided to face my fears head on and go. When we arrived in Juarez, the scent of Mexican laurel mixed with cilantro momentarily defended my sense of smell from the stench of rotting garbage. In the middle of a street lined with houses made of cardboard and pallets, my fear gave way to pride—I was here to share the wealth of God. The devil was dancing the rumba now.

My kidneys were not working optimally our first day out, and in the 100-degree weather, dehydration quickly set in. I knew something was wrong when I couldn't see anything but white shapes. Fear seized me. Should I have come? I panicked, and the devil danced the cha-cha.

Meagan, our nurse, ordered me to sit in the shade. As I sat in the cool and slowly recuperated, my fear began to settle, and the devil took five to rest his feet.

Color returned to the shapes around me. My fear turned to sober attention. Among the discarded tires and broken bottles, I saw children playing. A young boy scampered over, squatted, and stared curiously.

"¿Usted conoce a Jesús?" "Do you know Jesus?" is what I hoped I asked.

"¿Sí, usted?" he responded. My mind exploded with comprehension: "Yes, do you?"

In that moment, God had quieted the noise of my fear and pride. He allowed me to hear His whisper: *Find contentment with what I have given, for it is sufficient for My plan.*

Since returning from Juarez, God has healed me. The tumors are benign. My prideful soul has been replaced with a servant's heart as I realized that God did not send me to Juarez to be a super-servant, but to learn how to serve with humility. And the fear that crippled me subsided when I realized that though God's purposes might take me through danger, He would never leave me.

ACTION STEP

THE BEST WAY TO OVERCOME FEAR IS NOT THROUGH DWELLING ON THE FEAR, BUT BY FOCUSING POSITIVELY ON RESOURCES WE HAVE TO BE VICTORIOUS. WHAT GREATER RESOURCE IS THERE FOR YOU THAN GOD'S PRESENCE IN YOUR LIFE? FIND A SMALL STONE OR SOME OTHER TOKEN TO REMIND YOU THAT WITH GOD ALL THINGS ARE POSSIBLE. CARRY IT IN YOUR POCKET THIS NEXT WEEK—MAYBE LONGER—AND LET IT REMIND YOU OF GOD'S PRESENCE WHEN YOU FACE TOUGH SITUATIONS.

PRAYER

Dear God, You are my Rock, my Strength, my Shield, my Deliverer. With You I am ready for any battle of life!

DEALING WITH SETBACKS AND DETOURS

WHEN FACING DISAPPOINTMENTS AND ADVERSITY,
HOW WE HANDLE THEM IS MORE IMPORTANT
THAN THE DISAPPOINTMENTS THEMSELVES.

Fall seven times, stand up eight.

JAPANESE PROVERB

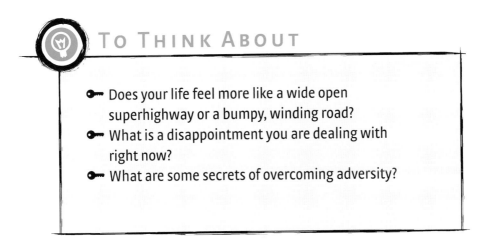

TO THINK ABOUT

- Does your life feel more like a wide open superhighway or a bumpy, winding road?
- What is a disappointment you are dealing with right now?
- What are some secrets of overcoming adversity?

LESSON FOR LIFE

PROMISES:

God will—

Fulfill His plans for you
Proverbs 19:21

Always be trustworthy
1 Peter 2:6

Give you satisfaction
in Him
Psalm 90:14

Care for you
Psalm 55:22

Rescue you in
tough times
Matthew 14:21

Stand Firm

BIBLE STUDY PASSAGE: HEBREWS 12:1-4

*We also have joy with our troubles, because we know
that these troubles produce patience.   And patience
produces character, and character produces hope.   And
this hope will never disappoint us, because God has
poured out his love to fill our hearts.   He gave us his love
through the Holy Spirit, whom God has given to us.*

ROMANS 5:3-5

We live in the age of instant gratification.   We look at our
teenagers and young adults and click our tongues because they
want only the best now—new cars, new clothes, new toys, and
lots of debt.   But they learned those values and attitudes
somewhere!

But perhaps even more disconcerting than an impatient,
acquisitive spirit is the refusal to pursue good, noble, worthy
dreams because they don't come soon, easy, or conveniently
enough.   Esau traded his family birthright for a bowl of soup
because he was hungry now (Genesis 25:29-34).   Saul lost his
kingship because of greed (1 Samuel 15:7-11) and fear of the

future (1 Samuel 28:7, 1 Chronicles 10:13). The rich young ruler sadly chose not to follow Jesus because the cost was too high (Luke 18:22-24).

Did you know that perseverance and failure cannot coexist? Why? Failure only happens when you quit. Whether it be a relationship, a spiritual issue, or a personal soul, as long as you keep trying, you are in the game.

The writer of Hebrews calls for his persecuted flock of Christians to "not get tired and stop trying" (12:3). He reminds them that in tough times, if we want to win the race, we must get rid of things that hinder us and sin that entangles us. We can't run with extra weight and cords around our ankles. But even more importantly, he calls all of us to keep our eyes on Jesus, the author and perfector of our faith, who showed us how to run the race with perseverance. When we see our final destination and know that others have gone before us, it makes even the difficult moments of the journey more than bearable.

Though there are accomplishments and spiritual growth that happen because of a quick spirit, the matters of greatest importance are usually more like a marathon. The good news is that Jesus runs beside us each step of the way.

"I say this because I know what I am planning for you," says the Lord. "I have good plans for you, not plans to hurt you. I will give you hope and a good future."
Jeremiah 29:11

REAL LIFE

My Life as a Reluctant Bus Driver

BRIAN KANNADY AS TOLD TO JESSICA INMAN

My sophomore year in college, I changed majors to enter the booming field of information technology. That year, people were leaving college before graduation to take highly lucrative jobs managing computer systems. I figured I would jump right into some cushy job after college.

Reality, however, did not match my undergrad hopes. The year I finished school, the IT field and the city I'd grown up in were in a deep slump, and I graduated without the dream job I'd expected.

And so August found me driving a bus route. Driving a school bus had been my college job (and source of funds for soda and pizza), so I was used to carting a busload of kids through their neighborhoods. Still, this wasn't exactly an exciting turn in my life.

Plus, I bore the special burden of having one of the toughest routes on the district. One afternoon during my sixth grade route, a man approached my window on foot and said that a rock flung from a window of my bus had broken his windshield.

I was grateful for my job—I really was. I knew that God had blessed me with income during the city-wide epidemic of unemployment. I tried to have patience, but that didn't change the fact that I really wanted to be doing something else. All through college, I had prayed so comfortably, knowing that God had a plan for my future. I guess I still knew that, but it just wasn't clear how His plan for my career would shape up.

It's not like I hadn't been looking for IT jobs. I had gone on a few interviews since graduation. At first, I wasn't worried. I felt confident that the right thing would come along. But when these openings bottomed out, I found myself praying urgently, *please, any non-bus job, ASAP.*

After a few months since my last interview, I landed an interview with a hospital IT department. This was a gleaming beacon, a lighthouse during the storm. Unfortunately, the interview didn't go very well—interviews are not my strong suit. So I was shocked when I received a second interview with the director, and shocked further when I got the job. Thirteen months after graduation, I finally had a job I wanted.

My last day as a bus driver, I marveled at how God had taken care of me for the last year. Not only did He make sure that I never missed a paycheck during my job hunt, but He taught me some valuable crisis management skills through a rowdy group of bus kids—and He brought me to a job that fit me perfectly. I'm really glad I trusted Him and let Him teach me about His faithfulness during my desert wandering as a bus driver.

ACTION STEP

IF LIFE IS MORE LIKE A MARATHON THAN A SPRINT, WHY NOT WALK OR RUN YOUR OWN PERSONAL MARATHON TODAY? NO, YOU DON'T HAVE TO COVER TWENTY-SIX MILES ON FOOT, BUT PLOT OUT A NICE, LONG, ONE-HOUR COURSE, AND SPEND THE TIME TALKING TO GOD ABOUT THE VARIOUS CHALLENGES YOU ARE FACING NOW, THANKING HIM FOR HIS HELP EACH STEP OF YOUR JOURNEY AHEAD, AND PRAISING HIM THAT HE LOVES YOU AND CARES ABOUT ALL AREAS OF YOUR LIFE.

PRAYER

Thank You, Heavenly Father, that no matter what challenges I face today and tomorrow, You provide me with the physical, emotional, and spiritual resources that I need.

FORGIVING MYSELF

GOD DOES NOT WANT US TO CARRY A LIFELONG LOAD OF GUILT ON OUR BACKS, BUT TO ACCEPT HIS FORGIVENESS AND MOVE ON.

Forgiveness does not change the past, but it does enlarge the future.

PAUL BOESE

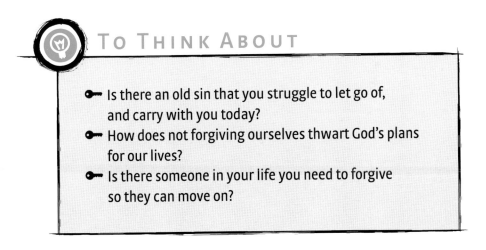

TO THINK ABOUT

- Is there an old sin that you struggle to let go of, and carry with you today?
- How does not forgiving ourselves thwart God's plans for our lives?
- Is there someone in your life you need to forgive so they can move on?

LESSON FOR LIFE

PROMISES:

God will—

Forgive you
Acts 10:43

Heal damaged emotions
Isaiah 57:18

Cleanse you
1 John 1:8-9
Colossians 2:34

Give you a new life
2 Corinthians 5:17

Forget your sins
Micah 7:19

God's Amazing Mercy

BIBLE STUDY PASSAGE: PSALM 51

God, be merciful to me because you are loving. Because you are always ready to be merciful, wipe out all my wrongs. Wash away all my guilt and make me clean again.

PSALM 51:1-2

You don't understand some of the things I've done. I'm not sure God can—or would even want to—forgive me.

Even the great heroes of the Bible had serious character flaws and were in need of God's mercy!

Jacob, the son of Isaac and one of the fathers of our faith, tricked his twin brother and even his beloved father, in order to "steal" the family birth right (Genesis 25-27).

Moses, who led the Hebrew slaves from the Pharaoh's oppression in Egypt, murdered a man and lived as a fugitive for forty years (Exodus 2-3).

David, perhaps the most beloved and popular of Israel's kings throughout history, performed many acts of courage, faith, and mercy—slaying the giant, Goliath, and sparing King Saul, a sworn enemy to him, to name just two—but also had a litany of sins and shortcomings strewn along his past.

His greatest crime was what he did to Uriah the Hittite, one of his bravest and most loyal soldiers. David coveted and then "took" Uriah's wife, Bathsheba, to be his own. To make his evil act even worse, he had Uriah killed to try and cover up what he had done. (See 2 Samuel 11-12 for the whole story.)

Throughout the Psalms, and especially in Psalm 51, David cries out for God's mercy. He knows that being the king doesn't get him off the hook. He knows that no act of contrition can undo his evil deeds.

There is no sin so great that God's grace is not greater. Be assured that God's mercy can and will enter a darkened heart and make it pure again.

I, I am the One who forgives all your sins, for my sake; I will not remember your sins.
Isaiah 43:25

REAL LIFE

I Was a Real Creep

ORVEY HAMPTON

After a few years of marriage, my wife and I were pretty disillusioned with life. We blamed each other. I worked at a job I hated and was bored. So one day I left her to search for greener pastures.

The first few weeks, I lavished myself with money borrowed from a bank. I played golf, partied at night, and slept in fashionable hotels. But every morning I thought about my pregnant wife and our four-year-old son. Playing golf helped me forget my troubles.

After a few weeks, the easy money ran out, and reality—and a dose of depression—began to set in. I got a job dealing cards in a casino and lived alone in an apartment. I resisted calling home for fear my wife had filed for divorce. I knew what a creep I had been.

One day the casino manager called me into his office. "Son, I have a letter from your wife," he said. "She didn't have your address. She said you walked out and left her penniless. Your baby is due in a few weeks. She's asked me to give you her letter. You need to grow up young man, go home, and get your life together. This is no way to live." He looked disgusted. You would have, too.

My face was beet red with humiliation as I walked out of his office.

But, looking back, I think the man was an angel. His words shook some sense into me! I dialed the phone and called my wife. I begged for forgiveness.

Understandably, she was skeptical, but she said she would try. During the next week, while earning money for a bus ticket home, I wrote many letters assuring her that I loved her.

But after we reconciled, our life was far from perfect! Then one day everything changed. A friend led my wife to a personal relationship with Jesus Christ. The change in her was apparent. I wanted what she had. Two months later I gave my life to Christ. He not only forgave me for all my sins, but He gave me a new beginning.

However, my past haunted me. I was burdened with guilt over what I had done to my family. Sometimes it would crop up during an argument. In time God led me to a mature Christian who explained what God's grace and forgiveness is all about. "But if we confess our sins, he will forgive our sins, because we can trust God to do what is right. He will cleanse us from all the wrongs we have done" (1 John 1:9).

"Orvey, we must take God at His Word," he said to me. "We cannot trust our feelings! You are forgiven because God said so!" That day I accepted God's unconditional forgiveness.

Soon my wife learned that God never keeps a list of our wrongs (1 Corinthians 13:5) though she had kept a list of mine. She was deeply convicted and asked God and me to forgive her for her *unforgiveness*. This year, we joyfully celebrate forty-three years of marriage. God is so good.

Forgiveness from others is charity; from God, grace; from oneself, wisdom.

ACTION STEP

IF THERE ARE PAST SINS THAT HAVE HAUNTED YOU—AND YOU HAVE TRULY ASKED GOD'S FORGIVENESS—THEN IT IS TIME TO MOVE ON. MAYBE A SYMBOLIC ACT WILL HELP MAKE FORGIVENESS MORE REAL TO YOU. WRITE DOWN THAT THING—OR THOSE THINGS—ON A SHEET OF PAPER. SAY A SHORT PRAYER, AND THEN LIGHT THE PAPER ON FIRE AND LET THAT SYMBOLIZE GOD'S ACT OF SCATTERING YOUR SINS AS FAR AS THE EAST IS FROM THE WEST.

PRAYER

Heavenly Father, thank You for saving my soul, forgiving me of my sins, and giving me a new life in You.

GRATITUDE

NOTHING WILL CHANGE YOUR PERSPECTIVE AND ATTITUDE ON LIFE MORE QUICKLY AND PROFOUNDLY THAN A SPIRIT OF GRATITUDE.

The Pilgrims made seven times more graves than huts.
No Americans have been more impoverished than these who,
nevertheless, set aside a day of thanksgiving.

H.U. WESTERMAYER

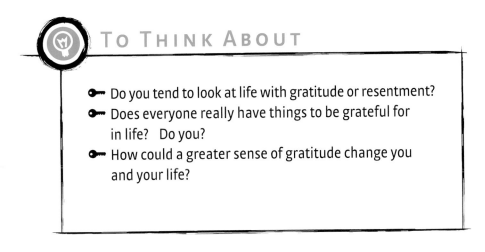

TO THINK ABOUT

- ⚬— Do you tend to look at life with gratitude or resentment?
- ⚬— Does everyone really have things to be grateful for in life?   Do you?
- ⚬— How could a greater sense of gratitude change you and your life?

LESSON FOR LIFE

PROMISES:

God will—

Bless you abundantly
Psalm 23:5

Bring you good things
Psalm 103:5

Gift good and
perfect gifts
James 1:17

Change the seasons
and give wisdom
Daniel 2:21

Give Thanks

BIBLE STUDY PASSAGE: PSALM 100

*Continue earnestly in prayer, being vigilant in it with
thanksgiving.*

COLOSSIANS 4:2

One of the lost arts of civility and friendship is the hand-written note.   It seemingly takes forever to write out a note of gratitude in a technologically advanced world where we can tap out a few letters—not necessarily spelled correctly—on our cell phone or laptop and send an instant message to our friends and family.   But the real tragedy is when we lose our sense of gratitude for others and God.

What happens when vibrant, active, kind, fun, difference-making individuals lose the wonder of gratitude?   Almost overnight you see a change of expression and feel the shrinking of the soul.

What is the cure for anger, bitterness, resentment, jeal-ousy, low self-esteem, a quarreling spirit, and other modern maladies? Simple. Express thanks! Instead of buying into the advertising of a consumer culture, we need to begin focusing on what we do have, not what we don't have.

In the one hundredth Psalm, King David leads his people in true worship. They are to honor God with glad hearts and joyful songs. Not only are they to have a thankful attitude, but they must say it aloud and "give thanks." David knows the real reasons for gratitude—

- *We have been created by God and belong to Him (100:3). The world is filled with arrogant people who only acknowledge themselves. But does this attitude really bring contentment and higher levels of self-actualization? It's not possible. Only when we acknowledge God do we discover our true selves.*
- *The Lord is good and His love endures forever (100:5). Does this mean that everything went right for David? Hardly. His life was filled with heartache and disappointment. There were times he lived in a state of depression and near despair. And yet, he understood that even in the "valley of the shadow of death" (Psalm 23:4), God was always near to comfort and bless him.*

Nothing will soothe the discomfort you may feel about your financial situation, marital status, or job difficulties like praising God for His goodness and blessings—and knowing that He has blessed you indeed.

Who gives food to all flesh, for His mercy endures forever. Oh, give thanks to the God of heaven! For His mercy endures forever.
Psalm 136:25-26 NKJV

85

REAL LIFE

Happy Thanksgiving

JAY COOKINGHAM

Growing up in rural New York State, I was exposed to what you might call rare delicacies. One of the more common entrées was the fuzzy gray speed bump known as squirrel. My father hunted for them frequently, which never seemed to me to be much of a feat. He would come back from hunting with a few gray pelts and act he was returning from some dangerous safari expedition. Our cat would catch one in the backyard, drop it at the front door, and be done with it, all the while looking at my father with pity.

We were quite poor and Dad's hunting provided the bulk of our meat. Squirrel stew graced our table frequently, and I ate it gratefully—sort of. However, on one Thanksgiving, that gray concoction would teach me an invaluable lesson.

That year, my family didn't have the money for anything close to a traditional turkey feast. My father's hunting forays hadn't produced much that fall, so whatever was still in our freezer would have to feed all eight of us. My mom had frozen some leftover squirrel stew months earlier, but on this holiday, that wasn't sounding very appetizing.

We tried to distract ourselves from our disappointment by watching the Macy's parade on our small black and white TV, but that only served as a big tease. In between the floats and balloons, commercials would show all the goodies many other families would enjoy that day. Even in black and white, the marshmallows, green bean casserole, and canned cranberry jelly looked scrumptious, and we smacked our lips hungrily. Curiously enough, though, not one of us kids asked, "Mom, when will dinner be ready?" in anticipation of the squirrel stew.

Around noon there was an unexpected knock at the front door. My mom opened the door to a sheepish and smiling man holding a huge box. When my mother let him in, he humbly placed the box on our dining room table. Wishing us a happy Thanksgiving, he left as quickly as he had come.

Inside the box were all the fixings for a hearty meal, including a large cooked turkey. I never found out where that man came from, but I did learn that God provides in the midst of any circumstances. I also realized that often I didn't become grateful until after God came through for me. The truth was that my heart needed to be grateful despite what was in (or not in) my stomach.

Now I look back with fondness and with laughter at those lean years with my family. I've discovered that how I choose to remember past events affects my level of everyday thankfulness. Those memories have taught me that whatever my situation, I always need to be thankful to God. I don't remember the taste of squirrel, but I do recall the provision He made for me that special happy Thanksgiving.

ACTION STEP

TAKE TIME TO WRITE SEVERAL THANK YOU NOTES: ONE TO A PERSON FROM YOUR PAST WHO HAS BLESSED YOUR LIFE; ONE TO A FAMILY MEMBER WHO PERHAPS YOU'VE BEEN TEMPTED TO TAKE FOR GRANTED; AND WRITE ONE LETTER TO GOD, THANKING HIM FOR HIS LOVE AND MERCY. TUCK THIS FINAL LETTER IN THE BACK OF YOUR BIBLE FOR FUTURE REFERENCE.

PRAYER

Thank You for who You are and all You have done for me, O God.

WISDOM

IN TOUGH TIMES, WE NEED TO TURN
TO GOD FOR A WISDOM THAT GOES
BEYOND HUMAN REASONING.

*The fear of the Lord, which is the beginning of wisdom,
consists in a complete devotion to God.*

OTTO ZOCKLER

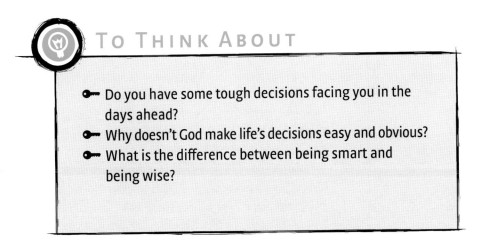

TO THINK ABOUT

- Do you have some tough decisions facing you in the days ahead?
- Why doesn't God make life's decisions easy and obvious?
- What is the difference between being smart and being wise?

LESSON FOR LIFE

PROMISES:

God will—

Give you wisdom
James 1:5

Direct your paths
Proverbs 3:5-6

Come to you when you
seek Him
Hosea 6:3

Care for you
1 Peter 5:7

Bless you as you
trust Him
Psalm 40:4

Wise Men

PROVERBS 3:1-16

He shows those who are humble how to do right, and he teaches them his ways.

PSALM 25:9

What does it take to be wise in today's world? More education? A better library? A new consultant? There are a lot of ways to grow in wisdom, but the Bible teaches a few key issues we would be unwise to ignore!

- *Wise men reverence God: "The fear of the Lord is the beginning of knowledge" (Proverbs 1:7 NKJV). The word that is translated "fear" in most English Bible translations is actually "reverence." How much respect do you show for God? In a culture that routinely uses God's name as an expletive, the wise man evidences awe of God in his words and heart.*
- *The wise man asks God for wisdom: "But if any of you needs wisdom, you should ask God for it. He is generous and enjoys giving to all people, so he will give you wisdom" (James 1:5). If you've been wondering what God wants you to do in life, your*

first step is to ask Him!

- Wise men "acknowledge" God (Proverbs 3:5-6). Many people take credit for the things that turn out great in life, but blame God when calamity strikes. Wisdom is understanding that all good gifts are from God (James 1:7)—and giving Him the credit. Acknowledging God also means we trust Him even when His plan doesn't make perfect sense to us.
- Wise men seek the counsel of godly people (Psalm 37:30). If you find yourself immersed in the thoughts of negative people who have no interest in serving God, you will be tempted to fall into their patterns of thinking. Who can you seek out who has a personal history of godly wisdom?
- Wise men get to know God's Word (Psalm 119:98). Some of our questions about God's direction for our lives would be cleared up immediately if we would do what King David practiced: "I will also meditate on all Your work, And talk of Your deeds" (Psalm 77:2 NKJV).

Are you facing a tough decision? Are you lacking wisdom? Turn to the Author of wisdom today!

Only the Lord gives wisdom; he gives knowledge and understanding.
Proverbs 2:6

REAL LIFE

"Dad, I'll Always Love You"

JOAN CLAYTON

Emmitt put aside his competency scores and attendance records. Being principal of a high school is a real challenge. His early morning quiet times with God brought solutions to the challenges, and those answers kept him going.

He was looking forward to going home, relaxing with his wife, Joan, and their sophomore son, Lane. The fact that Lane's dad was his principal didn't bring special treatment at school, but at home Lane was Emmitt's pride and joy.

"Dad, do you know what it's like to be the principal's son and have all the kids like my dad? Dad, I'll always love you." Those words are forever engraved in Emmitt's heart.

Emmitt drove into his driveway to discover Lane's red Monte Carlo filled with clothes.

"What's going on?" he asked as Lane came out of the house with an armload of stuff.

"I'm leaving home, Dad. I'm tired of school."

"Is this some kind of joke? You surely aren't serious!" Yet Lane was serious. Emmitt tried to reason with him, reminding him of the great future he had ahead and the possibilities of scholarships for college. How the situation would look to others didn't bother him—Lane was his son and, loving him dearly, Emmitt wanted his highest good.

Emmitt pleaded for hours, Joan crying all the while. "Please don't go," she begged, but Lane pulled away from her.

Please help me, Lord. I need wisdom. After that silent prayer, Emmitt felt a sense of peace. He felt in his heart God had said, "Let him go, and he will come back."

He took Lane in his arms and said, "We love you so and it hurts so bad, but our prayers for you will never stop."

"We can't do that," Lane's mother screamed. "He's only sixteen."

"We have invested love, truth, and prayers in him. Now we must put him in God's hands."

So Joan finally dried her eyes and kissed Lane goodbye. With broken hearts they watched Lane drive away as far as they could see.

That night Emmitt clung to the words and peace he had received in his earlier "emergency" prayer, trying to comfort Joan as she tossed and turned.

At 4:30 the next morning, he thought he heard a car pull up in the driveway. He went to the door to see his son. *Thank You, Lord—You brought our boy home.*

They hugged each other with a big bear hug. Lane swept his mother off her feet, saying, "I love you, Mom. The farther down the road I got, the more I realized I could leave home, but I couldn't leave love. Dad, I will always love you!"

Emmitt will never forget the night he had to decide what to do—quickly—and place his son in God's hands. As a principal and a dad, after that night, he'll never hesitate to trust in God's wisdom and faithfulness.

ACTION STEP

IF YOU ARE IN NEED OF GOD'S WISDOM ON A SPECIFIC ISSUE TODAY, SEEK OUT AN OLDER, WISER, GODLY MAN WITH WHOM YOU CAN DISCUSS THE MATTER IN CONFIDENCE. MEET SOMEWHERE, LIKE A QUIET COFFEE SHOP, WHERE YOU CAN SHUT OUT DISTRACTIONS.

PRAYER

God of all wisdom and power, I come to You today, asking for more faith, more godliness, and more wisdom.

WORKING WITH DIFFICULT PEOPLE

EVEN WHEN OTHERS CREATE STRIFE,
WE CAN DEMONSTRATE POISE AND
CHARACTER WITH GOD'S HELP.

Commitment in the face of conflict produces character.

UNKNOWN

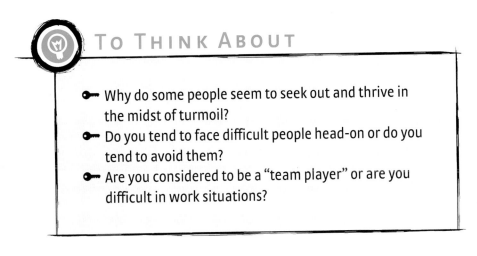

TO THINK ABOUT

- Why do some people seem to seek out and thrive in the midst of turmoil?
- Do you tend to face difficult people head-on or do you tend to avoid them?
- Are you considered to be a "team player" or are you difficult in work situations?

LESSON FOR LIFE

PROMISES:

God will—

Reveal himself to you
as you seek peace
and holiness
Hebrews 12:14

Bless you
Matthew 5:9

Defend you
Isaiah 41:11-12
Psalm 5:11

Give you wisdom
James 1:5

No Complaining or Arguing

BIBLE STUDY PASSAGE: PHILIPPIANS 2:12-15

I can do all things through Christ, because he gives me strength.

PHILIPPIANS 4:13

We're not surprised when we have to tell our children to stop complaining or arguing. After all, they're kids. But what's amazing is the number of "grownups" who can't seem to stop grumbling and stirring up trouble, even in the workplace.

Perhaps no one suffered more in the workplace than the great biblical character Joseph. Sold into slavery by his jealous brothers, he quickly moved up the ranks and became the head of the household for an Egyptian army captain named Potiphar (Genesis 37:36). When Joseph rebuffed the inappropriate advances of Potiphar's wife, she lied to her husband about him, and Joseph was thrown into prison (Genesis 39:20). While in prison, he again proved himself to be so reliable that the jailor enlisted him to assist in the work and gave him special privileges (Genesis 39:21-23). But even after giving wise counsel to several fellow prisoners, he was still forgotten and passed over for years (Genesis 40:23).

The good news for Joseph is that his faithfulness was finally rewarded. He rose to become the second most powerful man in Egypt, the undisputed superpower of its day (Genesis 41:40).

Conflict in the workplace is probably inevitable, though obviously handled better and worse depending on leadership and company culture. The temptation in difficult work environments is to practice an eye for an eye, and become just as difficult as the next person. Paul says that the truly successful person does everything "without complaining or arguing" (Philippians 2:14).

Even if you face temporary setbacks for doing what is right, in the long run, "the Lord watches over the lives of the innocent, and their reward will last forever" (Psalm 37:18).

If it is possible, as much as depends on you, live peaceably with all men.
Romans 12:18 NKJV

REAL LIFE

Staying the Course

AS TOLD TO JESSICA INMAN

In the sticky night air at a Promise Keepers rally, I prayed what I feared might be a dangerous prayer: I asked God to use me more. The speaker warned us that some things might come our way to keep us from making good on any commitment we made. What I didn't realize then was how crazy my life at work was about to become.

I had been promoted to director of rehab at an orthopedic hospital. I had previously worked on the same organizational level as a woman named Tina.* After my promotion, however, I became her boss. And she wasn't too thrilled about that.

At one point, she had gone to my boss with a list of accusations—alleging among other things that I left the building for hours at a time without explanation. My boss actually drew up my termination papers, but relented after I defended myself.

Things had gotten better—until the Tuesday I returned to work after Promise Keepers. Apparently, over the weekend, Tina decided that she wanted my job and was willing to do anything to get it.

She began a campaign of lies about me, telling anyone who would listen that I had committed Medicare fraud, something she knew would cost me my job—and possibly my state license.

I was nervous. But I knew God wanted me not to give in to the temptation to sling mud or gossip, no matter what happened—which wasn't easy, especially when she began to lie to my staff, which made daily work insufferably difficult.

After months of dealing with this situation, I went home one night and cried. I opened my Bible and through stinging eyes read in 1 Peter about suffering while doing what is right and entrusting ourselves to a "faithful Creator." I thanked God for giving me the encouragement I needed at precisely my weakest moment.

Slowly, people began to see inconsistencies between Tina's gossip and my behavior. My boss was among those who had watched me and found Tina's stories wanting. And when she began to lie about him as well, his belief in my innocence was cemented.

Before long, Tina was fired. My nightmare was over—I had been exonerated, and I no longer had to go to work not knowing what would happen that day.

During this experience, God didn't just protect my job, but also calmed my tired heart like a loving Father. The men's group at my church lifted so many prayers for me and offered strong arms across my shoulders, and God kept talking to me through people and Scripture.

After the storm had blown over, my coworkers told me how much it meant to them to see me stand firm, and the events fostered an atmosphere of faith in our office. God had answered my prayer and given me an opportunity to shine for Him, and He proved himself to be faithful to help me through any storm that may come my way.

*Names have been changed.

ACTION STEP

EVALUATE YOURSELF IN THE WORKPLACE IN THE FOLLOWING AREAS:

- FOLLOW THROUGH
- TEAM BUILDING
- RESPECT FOR LEADERSHIP
- MENTORING YOUNGER WORKS
- INTEGRITY AND HONESTY
- CUSTOMER CARE

WHAT ARE AREAS OF STRENGTH FOR YOU? IN WHAT AREAS DO YOU NEED TO GROW?

PRAYER

Lord God, forgive me for sometimes not being gracious toward my coworkers and supervisors. Help me reflect Your character at work, Lord.

LOVING YOUR WIFE

WHEN YOU LOVE YOUR WIFE AS CHRIST LOVES THE CHURCH, YOU EXPERIENCE A NEW LEVEL OF GOD'S GRACE IN YOUR SOUL.

To keep your marriage brimming,
With love in the loving cup,
Whenever you're wrong, admit it,
Whenever you're right, shut up.

OGDEN NASH

TO THINK ABOUT

- How would you characterize your relationship with your spouse today?
- Are there areas of concern you need to address?
- What can you do today to be a better husband and lover?

LESSON FOR LIFE

As Christ Loved the Church

BIBLE STUDY PASSAGE: EPHESIANS 5:21-33

*Pursue peace with all people, and holiness, without
which no one will see the Lord: looking carefully lest
anyone fall short of the grace of God; lest any root of
bitterness springing up cause trouble, and by this many
become defiled.*

HEBREWS 12:14-15 NKJV

In Ephesians 5:22, St. Paul says to wives: "Wives, submit to
your own husbands, as to the Lord" (NKJV). Many women have
read those words with great fear and anxiety, wondering if they
are being commanded to become doormats who meekly serve
their husbands. And a few men over the ages have used that
verse to rationalize harsh and overbearing treatment of their
wives. The key to understanding Paul's meaning here is one
verse earlier, where he says: "submitting to one another in the
fear of God" (Ephesians 5:21 NKJV).

In other words, the overriding principle for a great marriage
is mutual submission—a man and woman willingly, joyfully,
obediently putting the needs of their spouse before their own

needs. Just think how the state of marriage today would be enhanced if more couples would submit to one another.

But Paul doesn't stop there for men. In verse 25, he says: "Husbands, love your wives as Christ loved the church and gave himself for it." We all know how much Christ loved the church: He willingly died for His beloved.

So where do you start to love your wife like this, to build a fabulous marriage?

- *First and foremost, remember that love is a decision, not just a feeling. Decide today to speak and act with courtesy, kindness, affection, respect, and integrity. It's true that actions follow attitudes, but just as often, actions go before attitudes. If you want to feel more in love, act more in love!*
- *Second, flee from influences that would do damage to your marriage. If certain forms of media are causing you to unfavorably judge your wife, eliminate them. If certain people represent unhealthy temptation, don't spend time with them.*
- *Third, be sure to draw closer to God on a daily basis. The more you love God, the more you are able to love your spouse.*

May your soul—and your wife's soul—be changed for the better as you seek to love her extravagantly.

So a man will leave his father and mother and be united with his wife, and the two will become one body.

Genesis 2:24

REAL LIFE

The Power of a Confession

LARRY MILLER

Along with my retirement from law enforcement, my wife and I were dealing with moving away from family and friends, saying goodbye to our daughter who moved 3,000 miles away, and thousands of decisions about buying and decorating our new house. Stress was taking a toll on our relationship after thirty-two years of marriage.

When she mentioned that she wanted a concrete pad next to the house for the trash cans, I brusquely vetoed that idea since I'd already decided we would store them in the garage. When Kathy expressed how wounded she felt, I just turned away. She'd seemed a little oversensitive lately because of her peri-menopause—it seemed every time I offered an opinion, she took offense. If I attempted to explain, she reacted with silence or tears. It seemed like I couldn't say anything right, so why even try?

I half wanted to stop talking to her altogether because it hurt too much to see her in pain. Apologizing and talking out our conflicts used to bring intimacy—but not now!

I told myself, "Just gut this out until Kathy's hormones get settled. After all, it's her problem." I felt uneasy, though—we were marriage "experts," often sharing at couples' retreats and writing books about marriage. Was I handling this right?

One day, Kathy was away and I was reflecting on the most important theme I share in my speaking: the husband taking responsibility to lead. As I thought about the friction in our marriage, the Lord spoke to my heart, *Take responsibility.*

I realized that the real issue at hand wasn't Kathy's changed sensitivity, but my reluctance to take leadership. Immediately, I called Kathy and told her, "Honey, I need your forgiveness. I haven't been a leader when it comes to the struggles we've been having lately. This is not your problem—it's our problem and we'll do whatever it takes to work through this together."

After a somewhat frightening pause, Kathy said with a thickened voice, "Honey, you don't know how much that means to me. Thank you! I love you."

When I asked for Kathy's forgiveness, I proved to her that I was seeking the Lord and was sensitive to her—that I wanted to love her as He loved her. When she returned from her trip, she came back unburdened, the beautiful and happy woman I knew.

"Larry," she said as she hugged me, "I can't believe the difference I feel toward you."

I smiled and kissed her forehead, glad that my confession had set her free as I'd hoped it would.

We began to focus on the positives instead of the negatives in the new stresses we were facing in retirement. We both made a compromise or two. But most importantly, I continued to show my leadership proactively by telling her daily how much I loved and appreciated her.

Nothing has been better for our marriage than my decision to do the leading when it came to loving.

ACTION STEP

THIS SHOULD BE THE MOST FUN ACTIVITY IN THE *SOUL MATTERS FOR MEN* BOOK. PLAN A SPECIAL EVENING OUT WITH YOUR SPOUSE. IF YOU WERE ALREADY PLANNING THIS BECAUSE OF A BIRTHDAY OR ANNIVERSARY, PLAN ANOTHER, SEPARATE NIGHT. MAKE RESERVATIONS AT HER FAVORITE RESTAURANT. BUY FLOWERS. MAKE ALL THE PLANS FOR BABYSITTING IF YOU HAVE KIDS. READ—OR BETTER YET, MEMORIZE—A LOVE POEM TO SHARE OVER DINNER. TELL HER HOW BEAUTIFUL SHE IS AND HOW MUCH YOU LOVE HER THROUGHOUT THE EVENING.

PRAYER

Lord God, I remember today how amazing Your love is. Please give me the strength and character to love my wife the same way.

THE SUPPORT OF OTHERS

MANY MEN ARE TEMPTED TO FACE LIFE WITH ONLY THEIR OWN STRENGTH, BUT WE ALL NEED THE ENCOURAGEMENT AND SUPPORT OF OTHERS.

Insomuch as anyone pushes you nearer to God, he or she is your friend.

ANONYMOUS

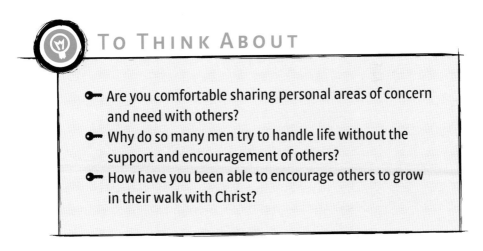

To Think About

- Are you comfortable sharing personal areas of concern and need with others?
- Why do so many men try to handle life without the support and encouragement of others?
- How have you been able to encourage others to grow in their walk with Christ?

LESSON FOR LIFE

PROMISES:

God will—

Fulfill the law of Christ as you build each other up
Galatians 6:2

Hear your prayers as you pray for each other
James 5:16

Unify His church
John 17:21

Use your faith to encourage others, and others' faith to encourage you
Romans 1:12

We Really Do Need Each Other!

BIBLE STUDY PASSAGE: GALATIANS 6:1-9

If one falls down, the other can help him up.   But it is bad for the person who is alone and falls, because no one is there to help.

ECCLESIASTES 4:10

In the sixth chapter of Galatians, Paul sets out some of the most practical principles for expressing love for one another found anywhere in the Bible.   But just because they are practical doesn't make them easy!

First, he tells us that we should be redemptive people, helping restore those who have been caught in a sin (v. 1).   He does caution you that as you reach out to help someone, be extra careful not to get trapped in sin yourself.

Second, Paul challenges us to love others unconditionally, without judgment and comparisons (v. 4).   Competition can be friendly and healthy, but when it consumes our relationships, the inevitable result is conflict.   How many marital and sibling relationships have been torpedoed by a spirit of striving rather than a spirit of pulling together?

Next, Paul urges us to help carry the "excessive weights" that others are forced to bear (v. 2). He does point out that each of us should carry our own "backpacks," so we aren't required to do everything for others (v. 5). But when someone has burdens that are bigger than any one person should handle alone, we are to step in to help.

Most importantly, Paul reminds us not to give up on loving others (v. 9). Sure, some people are unbelievably difficult to love, but if we don't lose faith in God's power to authentically change their lives, our steadfast persistence may be the very thing that makes the difference between them finding God's forgiveness and peace or never receiving God's grace in their hearts.

The result of how we relate to others is simple, according to Paul. He says, "People harvest only what they plant" (v. 7). When we sow love into others, we will ultimately receive love in return. And the truth is that we all need that kind of love for a healthy soul.

In the same way, we are many, but in Christ we are all one body. Each one is a part of that body, and each part belongs to all the other parts.

Romans 12:5

 ## REAL LIFE

A True Hope

JERRY LANE

I was the "perfect kid" growing up, a youth group staple and voted most likely to succeed in my high school. After college, though, my desire to go into ministry became replaced with a desire for things and status.

I was spending everything I made and had hooked up with the wrong people. Before long, I was involved with drugs. Though my relationship with drugs was brief, I sustained terrible damage, losing everything and ending up in total despair and depression.

Months of hopelessness drove me to take what should have been a lethal dose of an over-the-counter sleep aid. After four days of doubting that I would survive, the doctor announced that I was a miracle—I had no evidence of the overdose in my body.

As time passed, through the counsel of a brother in Christ and many prayers, I began to feel a spark of hope for my life. God was softening my heart.

Three years later, I moved to another city to start work and was feeling great. But after a couple of months, I crashed and became suicidal again. This time, even though my hope was threadbare, I knew in the back of my mind that God wanted me here for a reason.

I entered a Christian counseling clinic where I dealt with some tough issues, like the sexual abuse and divorce in my past—now compounded by the choices

I had made. Week after week, I sat in the pale waiting room, only barely holding onto hope for my life.

At the behest of my counselors, I went to a recovery program at a local church and was amazed at the worshipful atmosphere and the testimony that spoke to my heart. Plus, I felt accepted by everyone there.

I received the same treatment at a weekly Bible study for single guys at the same church. It's hard to go places when you're depressed, so I could have so easily fallen through the cracks. But a few of the guys just kept calling and e-mailing me. I thought surely they were on staff—but they were just regular guys doing what they were challenged to do.

With continued counseling, lots of prayer, and the unwavering support of my church community, I became stronger. My bad days got better and farther apart. Before long, I was no longer crippled by depression.

God brought about a miraculous healing in my life, and He chose to use the prayers and encouragement of His people at this church and in my hometown. Here was a group of real, authentic people who were steadfast through the storms of life, even if the storms were not their own. They were truly ministers of the gospel, and through their love they strengthened my feeble knees—and led me to the Source of true hope.

ACTION STEP

ARE THERE ONE OR TWO MEN IN YOUR CIRCLE WHOSE BURDENS YOU CAN STEP UP TO CARRY? OR IS THERE A NEED IN YOUR LIFE YOU NEED TO SHARE WITH SOMEONE ELSE? TAKE A STEP TODAY—MAKE A PHONE CALL OR SEND AN E-MAIL TO OFFER PRAYERS OR REQUEST PRAYERS, OR BOTH. THEN WRITE ON YOUR CALENDAR OR IN YOUR PALM ONE THING YOU CAN DO TO HELP THAT PERSON OR THOSE PEOPLE WITH THE THINGS THEY'RE FACING.

PRAYER

God, thank You that You didn't create us to live in isolation, but to help each other seek and find You. Show me who to reach out to today.

THE POWER OF ATTITUDE

THE QUALITY OF OUR LIFE IS MORE DEPENDENT ON OUR PERSPECTIVE THAN OUR CIRCUMSTANCES.

A happy person is not a person in a certain set of circumstances,
but rather a person with a certain set of attitudes.

HUGH DOWNS

TO THINK ABOUT

- How do you feel when you are around someone who has a consistently negative, critical, cynical attitude? Do you ever notice?
- Are there some negative attitude issues in your life? How would you like to improve your attitude? What are some strengths you can build on?

LESSON FOR LIFE

PROMISES:

God will—

Renew your mind
Hebrews 8:10

Perfect your character
through patience
James 1:4

Give you patience and
renew your soul
2 Corinthians 4:16

Give you peace and rest
Isaiah 26:3

Hallmarks of a Great Attitude

BIBLE STUDY PASSAGE: PHILIPPIANS 2:3-11

Do not be interested only in your own life, but be interested in the lives of others.

PHILIPPIANS 2:4

Have you ever suffered from a stinky enough attitude that you didn't even want to be around yourself? A negative, critical, harsh, cynical attitude is poison to relationships—and to your soul.

If you're suffering from a bad case of negativity, here are some ideas to foster a winning attitude:

- *Smile: "Be full of joy in the Lord always. I will say again, be full of joy" (Philippians 4:4). Our countenance is often a reflection of what we're feeling inside. Even if you don't feel happy inside, fake it until you feel it.*
- *Say "thank you" often—"Let the peace that Christ gives control your thinking, because you were all called together in one body to have peace. Always be thankful" (Colossians 3:15). When we take others for granted and see only their faults, our attitude toward them—and theirs toward us—will go downhill fast. Express appreciation.*

- *Forgive fast: "Do not let the sun go down on your wrath" (Ephesians 4:26 NKJV). Unresolved anger and grudges cause us to hurt others—and ourselves. Work things out right now. Jesus says don't even go to church without clearing things up with your brother (Matthew 5:23-25).*
- *Be proactive—"Let us think about each other and help each other to show love and do good deeds" (Hebrews 10:24). Instead of moaning and groaning and complaining about how bad things are, act. Inaction is a breeding ground for negativity. Don't like the yard? Organize a work day and gently but firmly enlist the support of your family. Keep smiling.*
- *Watch your words—"When you talk, do not say harmful things, but say what people need" (Ephesians 4:29). What we say has a tremendous impact on how we feel. Do your words make you more or less positive?*
- *Cheer up someone else: "By helping each other with your troubles, you truly obey the law of Christ" (Galatians 6:2). Find someone who really has problems, and help them see life through the eyes of faith and hope again. It will help you, too.*

A great attitude won't change your circumstances—but it will change the way you experience life. Rejoice. Your new attitude begins today!

In your lives you must think and act like Christ Jesus.
Philippians 2:5

115

REAL LIFE

A Server of Blessings

GINGER COX

It was one of those days of spinning wheels. Sam had driven 540 long miles, was disappointed with business appointments, and felt exhausted. Hungry and discouraged, he walked into a restaurant, ready for a nourishing meal to lift his deflated spirit. Yet it wasn't just the food that would fill him that night.

A waiter appeared, flashing a bright smile as he escorted Sam to a table. "Hi! I'm Leon, and I'll be your server tonight. How are you?"

Sam responded nonchalantly, "Fine, and how about you?"

"Blessed," said Leon with his cheerful grin. "God is good." Wondering about this unusual response, Sam settled into his seat, watching as Leon busily and attentively moved from table to table. A departing family left a huge mess, but Leon smiled as he quickly cleaned the table for new diners.

As Leon brought hot rolls to the table, Sam motioned to him. "Leon, stop a minute so I can ask you a question. How in the world can you be so cheerful?"

Showing his gold-capped teeth with a huge grin, Leon immediately shared his belief in the grace of God. There was no doubt about the source of his enthusiastic joy. His Scripture references were accurately on target, launched straight from the heart.

Throughout the meal and between jaunts to other tables, Leon stopped to answer more thought-provoking questions from Sam. Leon depended on tips, but they had no bearing on his work ethic. Left with either a tip or a mess, Leon praised God and worked hard.

While serving Sam complimentary coffee, Leon told him about his former drug problem and shared his deep compassion for others still caught in that lifestyle. Sam also learned Leon's fiancée had a serious thyroid problem. "What is her name—for prayers?" Sam asked.

Leon quickly wrote on a slip of paper. "Here are our full names, but He knows who we are."

Sam usually left tips on dining tables, but this evening he handed his directly to Leon. Looking him straight in the eye, Sam added, "Thanks, Leon. You don't know how much I appreciate your service tonight."

Leon flashed his golden smile, leaned close, and confided quietly, "Church people are often the worst tippers." Then he stood tall and said, "But God knows what is happening, and He keeps blessing me. Just like having you here tonight!"

After the spirit-filled meal, Sam left for his last business appointment of the day. Not surprisingly, it turned out to be one of his most successful contacts of the weeklong trip.

In 1 Peter 3:15, it says, "Always be ready to answer everyone who asks you to explain about the hope you have."

Saint Peter, you would be proud! Leon continues your work, par excellence.

ACTION STEP

ATTITUDE IS SO FOUNDATIONAL TO THE QUALITY OF LIFE WE LIVE THAT MAYBE WE NEED TO GET BACK TO BASICS. BEFORE YOU LAUGH THIS ACTIVITY OFF AS TOO SIMPLE, ASK YOURSELF: HOW BAD DO I NEED A BETTER ATTITUDE?

GO TO A CRAFT STORE OR THE SCHOOL SUPPLIES SECTION OF ANOTHER RETAIL OUTLET. BUY NOTECARDS AND STICKERS—ESPECIALLY GOLD STARS. LABEL A NOTECARD FOR EVERY DAY OF THIS COMING WEEK. EVERY TIME YOU EXPRESS A POSITIVE ATTITUDE, ADD A BRIGHT, COLORFUL, HAPPY STICKER TO THE CARD. WHEN YOU EXPRESS A NEGATIVE ATTITUDE, ADHERE A FROWNING FACE OR OTHER SAD STICKER.

AT THE END OF THE WEEK, TAKE A LOOK AND SEE HOW YOU'RE DOING.

PRAYER

Father, help me enjoy the wonderful things You've given me by having a great attitude.

GOD'S DISCIPLINE

GOD ALLOWS CHALLENGES— AND EVEN PAIN—INTO OUR LIVES TO BUILD GODLY CHARACTER WITHIN US.

God allows pain because he is more interested in your character than your comfort.

RICK WARREN

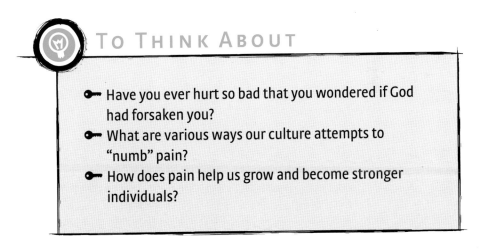

TO THINK ABOUT

- Have you ever hurt so bad that you wondered if God had forsaken you?
- What are various ways our culture attempts to "numb" pain?
- How does pain help us grow and become stronger individuals?

LESSON FOR LIFE

PROMISES:

God will—

Strengthen you
through trials
James 1:3

Bless you through
discipline
Psalm 94:12

Be near to you in all
circumstances
Psalm 145:8

Work all things for your
ultimate good
Romans 8:28

No Pain, No Gain

BIBLE STUDY PASSAGE: HEBREWS 12:1-12

*The Lord disciplines those he loves, and he punishes
everyone he accepts as his child.*

HEBREWS 12:6

No pain—no gain. We understand that little phrase when
we are at the gym working out. But it's a whole other story when
we—or someone we love—faces unavoidable physical or
emotional pain.

So does God hurt us in order to make us stronger? We know
for sure that God doesn't tempt us (James 1:13), but He does
allow trials to enter into our lives. The writer of Hebrews says we
should "hold on" during our sufferings "because they are like a
father's discipline" (12:7).

The writer of Hebrews calls for his persecuted flock of
Christians not to "get tired and stop trying" (12:3). He reminds
them that in tough times, if we want to win the race, we must get
rid of things that hinder us and sin that entangles us. We can't
run with extra weight and cords around our ankles. But even
more importantly, he calls all of us to keep our eyes on Jesus, the

author and perfector of our faith, who showed us how to run the race of life with perseverance (12:4). When we see our final destination and know that others have gone before us, it makes even the difficult moments of the journey more than bearable.

Here are a few reminders to bolster your soul when you experience pain in your life—

- *God will not allow anything to happen to you that you cannot bear (1 Corinthians 10:13).*
- *God is able to transform painful experiences into profound and powerful life lessons (Romans 8:28).*
- *God uses those who have experienced pain to bring comfort to others who are hurting today (2 Corinthians 1:4).*
- *God's eternal rewards far outweigh any suffering we experience today (Romans 8:18, 2 Corinthians 4:17).*
- *God is kind and loving and His ultimate plans for your life are for health, peace, and prosperity—and for those whose lives are cut short by martyrdom or service to God, even greater eternal rewards await them (Matthew 5:12, Revelation 14:13).*

God wants only what's best for us—but He knows that sometimes the only road to character is through pain. The good news is that Jesus runs beside us each step of the way.

The Lord has mercy on those who respect him, as a father has mercy on his children. He knows how we were made; he remembers that we are dust.
Psalm 103:13-14

 REAL LIFE

The Nail

MAX DAVIS

It was my daughter Kristen's tenth birthday party, and I was about to understand God just a little bit better.

For the party, some relatives had hung balloons on nails around our front porch. One of the balloons was the thick latex type, with a heavy-duty rubber band.

My eight-year-old, James, wanted a balloon—that balloon. He grabbed it and pulled, stretching the rubber band. Suddenly, the nail dislodged, the rubber band catapulting it directly into James's chest.

It wasn't pretty—the nail had lodged into the bone so deep that we thought he might die. Someone called 911, and a team of paramedics soon strapped James onto a gurney and whisked him away. They wouldn't allow me to ride in the ambulance with my son. James watched in terror, screaming for me to come.

You see, my son is totally deaf. What must have gone through his mind during that ambulance ride? Why has Daddy left me?

In the ER, the doctor told me, "For someone as young as James, surgery might cause further complications. We need to get the nail out now." He looked squarely at me. "It's going to be painful. But it's for the best."

The doctor instructed me to hold my son down while he attempted to remove the nail. Each time he even touched it, the pain would send James jerking and screaming. The doctor took a pair of pliers and started pulling, but it wouldn't budge. James couldn't talk, but his eyes pierced through me and said it all: "Daddy, do something. Don't let the doctor hurt me." I too was in tears and, in a moment of weakness, I let go.

I wondered whether I should stop everything and request surgery—I certainly could. But my instincts as a father told me that this was best. So, I took a deep breath and wrapped my arms around James. His eyes screamed, "Dad, how could you betray me? You know how this is hurting me. Do something!"

Yet all I could do was hold him down. This time, the doctor straddled James and used his legs for more power. Finally, the nail popped out. James and I sat there, exhausted and emotionally spent. James looked at me as if to say, "Daddy, why did you let them do that to me?" All I could do was hold him in my arms and love him.

Only another parent can understand the torment I was in at that moment. Just as God has the power to step into our lives and say, "Enough is enough," I had had the power to stop James' pain, but I didn't—because I knew that would ultimately be more harmful to him.

It may be awhile before James understands that, and it may be a while before I understand why God has brought discipline into my life the way He has. How many times have I looked at God the way James looked at me, feeling betrayed and confused?

When the ordeal was over, all James could do was sit on the doctor's table and be loved by me. And all I can do is remember that as I hurt for my son, God hurts for me, and be loved by Him.

ACTION STEP

St. Paul tells us that "training your body helps you in some ways, but serving God helps you in every way by bringing you blessings in this life and in the future life, too" (1 Timothy 4:18). As a reminder that discipline is one of the ways to build and strengthen the soul, plan a week of challenging yourself physically—light running or walking; pushups; sit-ups; stretching. Make a point to use this time to pray and meditate on Scripture.

PRAYER

Dear Heavenly Father, I know that You are good and work all things for good for me, even the hard things. Help me get the most out of the trials You've brought in my life today.

OVERCOMING FEELINGS OF INADEQUACY

GOD GIVES US ALL THE SPIRITUAL AND PERSONAL RESOURCES WE NEED TO BE CONFIDENT AND SUCCESSFUL.

Panic at the thought of doing a thing is a challenge to do it.

HENRY S. HASKINS

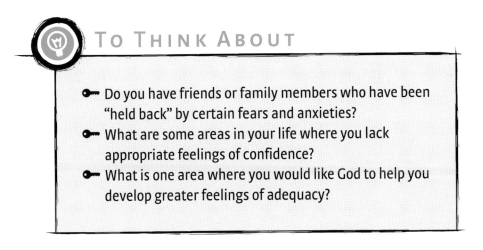

TO THINK ABOUT

- Do you have friends or family members who have been "held back" by certain fears and anxieties?
- What are some areas in your life where you lack appropriate feelings of confidence?
- What is one area where you would like God to help you develop greater feelings of adequacy?

LESSON FOR LIFE

PROMISES:

God will—

Make you a conqueror
Romans 8:37

Be trustworthy
1 Peter 1:21

Cause you to flourish
Jeremiah 17:7-8

Use your gifts
Ephesians 4:11

Give you the power you
need to succeed
Proverbs 16:3

My God Shall Supply

BIBLE STUDY PASSAGE: EXODUS 4:1-17

But Moses said to the Lord, "Please, Lord, I have never been a skilled speaker. Even now, after talking to you, I cannot speak well. I speak slowly and can't find the best words." Then the Lord said to him, "Who made a person's mouth? And who makes someone deaf or not able to speak? Or who gives a person sight or blindness? It is I, the Lord."

EXODUS 4:10-11

Though our society appropriately and sometimes inappropriately stresses self-actualization, self-confidence, and even self-aggrandizement, the sad truth is many of us suffer from feelings of inadequacy and are fearful about testing our wings and attempting to accomplish all that God has enabled us to do.

If you ever struggle with healthy self-confidence, note that one of the greatest leaders in all of history, Moses, had the same hang-up. When God called him to lead the children of Israel out of Egyptian bondage, Moses was full of excuses. *They won't listen to me. I stutter. Send my brother.* Maybe it was the trauma of separation from his parents as a baby and being adapted into a "foreign" culture. Maybe it was discovering his minority status as a young man. Maybe it was the guilt of moral failure as a young man or being raised as a prince while his own family served as slaves when he was a child. Whatever the reasons, Moses had tremendous feelings of inadequacy.

But God was patient with him. And Moses did step out on faith to face the Pharaoh and help forge a free nation as he took to heart God's promise to him: "I will help you speak, and I will teach you what to say" (Exodus 4:12).

Are you fearful? Do you feel inadequate to apply for a better job? Or volunteer to lead a small group? Or go back to school to get that degree? Or share God's love with a neighbor? Have feelings of inadequacy made your soul smaller? If God lays a new challenge on your heart, be assured He has already given you all the resources you need to be successful!

I can do all things through Christ, because he gives me strength.
Philippians 4:13

 REAL LIFE

Facing the Thing I Fear

TERRY BURNS

As a kid I was bashful and shy, tremendously so. I still am. My wife even has to order the pizza and return things to the store.

I had a teacher that recognized my problem and said that the answer was to groom my leadership skills. Leadership? How do you lead somebody when you can't even talk to them?

He started treating me as if I were the class leader, even suppressing the natural leaders a little to make it happen. He called on me a lot during class, and always made sure whatever I said turned out well. It gave me a little confidence. While I still had trouble in one-on-one settings, I discovered that a group was kind of faceless—I could talk in front of a group.

I started acting as if I was a leader, and believe me, it was a pure act at first. When I faced a confrontation or speaking to people, I pretended I wasn't afraid, and got through it. I faked confidence in leading groups for years—and somewhere along the way, I quit acting. I eventually became a chamber of commerce manager, spending over twenty-five years doing on a daily basis the thing I used to fear the most: speaking to groups.

Then came a life-changing revelation: I could write. As I worked on fanning into flame my gift of writing, I suddenly had a new idea: writing fiction. I wanted to write fiction, and I wanted my faith to be in the words, but as usual I was scared to try. I did what I've done so much of my life: I prayed about it. "God, do You want me to write, and do You want me to put a message in what I write?"

That same day, a brochure about a Christian writing conference came in the mail. Probably a coincidence, I reasoned. Plus, it cost too much to go. When my wife came home, I told her about the conference, and she got a funny look on her face. It turned out that earlier in the day she had gotten an unexpected check for some back work that was almost exactly the amount of money needed to go to the conference. This was amazing, but I was still scared to try.

That Sunday, our pastor preached about special gifts, and our Sunday school lesson fell along those lines as well. And as the week progressed, other confirmations arrived that I needed to go to the writing conference and take a step toward my dream of writing faith-filled novels and short stories.

When we pray to God, we need to be prepared for Him to repeat His answer until we really get it. He pushed me into going to that workshop and through it He spurred me to write more and keep writing. And I'm not sure I would have been able to hear Him and follow the dreams He gave me if my teacher hadn't taught me to face the thing I fear—which makes me think God placed that teacher in my life with a specific purpose.

Throughout my life, I've seen over and over again the amazing truth that God doesn't ask us to do anything He doesn't prepare and equip us to do.

ACTION STEP

WHAT IRRATIONAL—OR EVEN RATIONAL—FEAR IS HOLDING YOU BACK? ARE YOU AFRAID TO SPEAK IN A CROWD? MEET NEW PEOPLE? FLY IN AN AIRPLANE?

DETERMINE THIS WEEK TO TAKE A BABY STEP IN THE DIRECTION OF OVERCOMING YOUR FEAR. WRITE DOWN YOUR FEAR ON A NOTE CARD. NEXT TO IT, WRITE ONE TANGIBLE, ACTIVE STEP YOU CAN TAKE THIS WEEK. BE IN PRAYER THROUGHOUT THE WEEK, AND BE SURE TO FOLLOW THROUGH. AFTER YOU'VE TAKEN THAT BABY STEP, ASK GOD WHAT HE WANTS YOU TO DO NEXT.

PRAYER

Lord God, thank You that You equip us with everything we need to do Your will. Lord, challenge me with tasks that seem beyond what I am capable of doing, so that I can rely on You all the more.

THE ART OF GETTING ALONG

IT IS FINE TO SPEAK YOUR MIND AND BE TRUE TO YOUR HEART, BUT LOOKING FOR QUARRELS IS DESTRUCTIVE TO ALL.

I never take my own side in a quarrel.

ROBERT FROST

TO THINK ABOUT

- Do you have friends or acquaintances who always seem to be in the middle of a heated argument?
- Do you tend to be an accommodator who helps everyone get along—or do you tend to "mix it up"?
- Have you hurt some relationships due to a contentious spirit?

LESSON FOR LIFE

PROMISES:

God will—

Bless your obedience
Psalm 119:2

Make things go well
with you
Jeremiah 7:23

Make you shine
Philippians 2:14-15

Reward your efforts at
keeping peace
Matthew 5:9

Punish the quarrelsome
Proverbs 6:16-19

Be Gentle to All

BIBLE STUDY PASSAGE: ACTS 15:36-40

*And a servant of the Lord must not quarrel but must be
kind to everyone, a good teacher, and patient.*

2 TIMOTHY 2:24

No matter how kind, patient, peaceful, and godly you are, it is
impossible to avoid all conflicts. That's probably a good thing.
Sometimes disagreements in groups or between individuals can be
healthy and lead to significant growth and new understandings.

The Bible is filled with conflicts caused by flawed individuals.
Many conflicts led to tragic results, such as Cain murdering his brother
Abel (Genesis 4:8). Others were resolved with grace and restoration.

In the early church, Paul was the undisputed leader of spreading
the gospel. Just before launching on his second missionary journey, he
and his trusted colleague, Barnabas, had a sharp disagreement
regarding one of the team members. Young John Mark had deserted
them on their first trip, and Paul wasn't ready to offer a second chance.
Barnabas felt that the young man had grown up and was ready to be
trusted. The conflict reached impasse, and Paul and Barnabas went
separate ways.

The good news is that they doubled their impact, were later reconciled and worked together again, and in his last days, Paul even reached out to John Mark as a son.

How do you handle conflict? Arguments? Avoidance? Remember—

- *Attack problems—not people. You don't have to agree with someone to act with civility and Christian love.*
- *Don't allow ego to make you difficult. How many men have ship-wrecked their careers and relationships because they magnified a real or perceived slight to their dignity?*
- *Let conflict help you sort out what really matters. Why argue over petty issues? Hold your ground on what's important.*
- *Be quick to apologize, forgive, and move on when situations get highly contentious. Grudges hurt everyone, including you.*
- *Be open to new ideas and new ways of doing things. A little more humility and a little less argumentativeness may allow you grow.*

Some conflict can't be avoided, but a mature man uses conflict to further relationships, not break them down. The more you approach conflict by putting others' interests above your own (Philippians 2:3), the more the conflict will be fruitful—and your soul will flourish.

Love is patient and kind. Love is not jealous, it does not brag, and it is not proud. Love is not rude, is not selfish, and does not get upset with others. Love does not count up wrongs that have been done. Love is not happy with evil but is happy with the truth. Love patiently accepts all things. It always trusts, always hopes, and always remains strong.

1 Corinthians 13:4-7

133

REAL LIFE

My Beautiful Long Hair

LARRY KARR AS TOLD TO LAROSE KARR

One Friday in high school, I was called into the principal's office and told I would have to get my hair cut. At the time, it was just touching my collar and since I had been told the Supreme Court made it illegal to tell someone how to wear his or her hair, I balked.

The principal then brought out a Bible and said, "In here it says it's a sin for a man to have long hair. Don't come back to school without a haircut."

I laughed and said, "If anything, my hair will be a bit longer after the weekend." Not surprisingly, I dropped out of school a little while later.

My hair was down to my waist when I met my wife. You may be laughing, but man, I was proud of my long hair. I was never going to cut it.

After ten years of marriage, I began going to church with my wife and kids. I had accepted Christ one morning while watching a religious program at home.

With that commitment to God, I also made a decision to read the Bible from cover to cover. I started at Genesis, Exodus, and Leviticus, finally making it past Chronicles and all the begats to the New Testament. All the while, I was looking for that scripture about long hair that my high school principal had talked about. I don't think that was my main motivation, but it sure was on my mind.

I finally found it. I learned my principle had misquoted the verse in 1 Corinthians 11:14, which says, "Does not even nature itself teach you that if a man has long hair, it is a dishonor to him?" (NKJV). Hmmm. I wasn't positive what that meant. So I paid close attention to the scriptures that followed: "But if a woman has long hair, it is a glory to her; for her hair is given to her for a covering. But if anyone seems to be contentious, we have no such custom, nor do the churches of God" (1 Corinthians 11:15-16).

In other words, long hair was a matter of custom, not sin. The principal had misused the verse with me. Ha! My hair was safe. But something in the verses started gnawing at me. And for the next seven weeks I struggled with making a life-changing decision. Finally I came to peace with what I had to do.

I walked into the local beauty college with my hair flowing down to the back of my knees. I had untied the braid I usually wore. The students and teachers looked at me in astonishment. They could not believe I was going to let them cut my hair. Students, teachers, and other customers gathered around. They took pictures. Before proceeding, they carefully braided my hair and then cut off the braid so I could take it home.

I keep the braid in a box as a reminder. You see, the Bible liberated my heart. Instead of telling me that I could not wear long hair, the Scriptures taught me that the real issue is being contentious. And, man, was I contentious. I was always at odds with someone.

When I walked out of the beauty college that day with short hair I felt a heavy weight was lifted off my shoulders—literally and spiritually—because I finally knew the area of my heart that needed to change. With the help of God's Word, I no longer wanted to be a contentious man!

ACTION STEP

NEXT TIME YOU FIND YOURSELF IN A DEBATE AT HOME, WORK, CHURCH, OR OTHER SETTING, LET THE OTHER PERSON TALK FIRST: ASK THEM WHAT THEY THINK ARE THE MOST IMPORTANT ISSUES AT HAND, TURN TO FACE THEM, LOOK THEM IN THE EYE, AND DON'T INTERRUPT UNTIL THEY'RE THROUGH. THEN GENTLY EXPLAIN WHAT YOU AGREE WITH AND DISAGREE WITH.

WHEN THE CONVERSATION IS OVER, TAKE NOTES TO REMIND YOURSELF HOW YOU HANDLED IT—WHAT YOU SAID THAT HELPED SOOTHE ANY ANGER OR WHAT YOU SAID THAT AGGRAVATED THE SITUATION. COMMIT YOUR NOTES TO GOD AND ASK HIM TO HELP YOU LOVE THE PEOPLE AROUND YOU.

PRAYER

Heavenly Father, when I was Your enemy, You reconciled with me. Help me be a messenger of Your peace.

MENTORSHIP

TO REACH OUR FULL POTENTIAL, WE ALL
NEED A MENTOR—AND WE ALL NEED TO BE
A MENTOR FOR SOMEONE ELSE.

When the student is ready, the teacher will appear.

CHINESE PROVERB

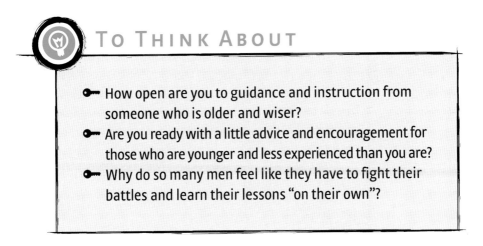

TO THINK ABOUT

- How open are you to guidance and instruction from someone who is older and wiser?
- Are you ready with a little advice and encouragement for those who are younger and less experienced than you are?
- Why do so many men feel like they have to fight their battles and learn their lessons "on their own"?

LESSON FOR LIFE

PROMISES:

God will—

Give you the Spirit as a
guide and teacher
John 14:16

Make you wise
James 1:5

Put leaders in your life
Jeremiah 3:15

Prepare you to
bless others
Hebrews 13:21

Live and Learn

BIBLE STUDY PASSAGE: 1 TIMOTHY 1:1-10

If you love someone, you will be loyal to him no matter what the cost. You will always believe in him, always expect the best of him and always stand your ground in defending him.

1 CORINTHIANS 13:7 TLB

It was Will Rogers, the famous cowboy philosopher and humorist, who said: "Experience may be the best teacher, but sometimes it's better to let the other guy get bit by the snake."

Women claim that men are genetically challenged when it comes to asking for directions. Their proof is missed turns and Christmas presents that are missing key parts when assembled the night before. And though we chuckle at such generalizations about our gender, the reality is that we sometimes choose to have less and be less because we are unwilling to seek out the counsel and wisdom of those who are wiser and have more experience than we do.

We don't know much about Timothy from his own words, but from Paul's letters to him in the New Testament, we discover he deeply appreciated his godly heritage (1 Timothy 1:5), he carefully followed the teaching of his mentor (1 Timothy 1:19), and as a result, he was wise beyond his years as a minister and leader (1 Timothy 4:12).

To be a great leader, you must be willing to be a great follower. An exhausted, ineffective, frustrated Moses could not keep up with the demands of leading his people—until he listened to the counsel of his father-in-law (Exodus 18:24). That takes humility and courage!

Bottom line, we would all do better if we had a trusted mentor in our lives, and that won't happen until our hearts are open and we are humble enough to learn from someone else.

If you want to start your own business, find someone who has already started one. If you want to grow spiritually, look for a man of spiritual grace and joy. If you want to be a better husband, watch a mature, loving husband and his little courtesies and affections. And then pass along what you've learned to others!

My children, listen to your father's teaching; pay attention so you will understand.
Proverbs 4:1

 REAL LIFE

Billy's Pecan Pie

DAVID KILBY AS TOLD TO KAREN KILBY

What would we have done without Billy's pecan pie? Not that it was needed as a staple for our diet—it was everything the pie represented that made the difference in our lives.

"Come on over for dinner," Karen's new friend, Eleanor, invited. "I want you to meet my husband, Bill. You'll love his southern cooking, especially a slice of his warm pecan pie topped with a mountain of ice cream!"

Bill and Eleanor could have offered us cheese and crackers and we would have been delighted to accept their invitation. With my unemployment, we needed all the encouragement we could get. These new friends from church seemed to sense that. Along with that generous slice of pecan pie a la mode came many evenings of generous amounts of love and concern, carrying us through times of triumph and trials over the next five years.

When I finally found employment, they were ecstatic for us. When I decided to leave the company and venture out on a dream of my own, they cheered me on. When my dream fell apart, they were there to comfort us, each time offering us another generous slice of Billy's pecan pie accompanied by their love and the reminder that neither defeat nor success is ever final.

Bill and Eleanor were gracious givers, each in their own way. Eleanor was a charming, genteel lady who loved setting the table with her fine china and sterling silver, making Billy's "home cookin'" taste even better! On several occasions, they would treat us to dinner at one of their favorite Sarasota restaurants or the Yacht Club. As a retired dentist, Bill seemed to know everyone in town. He enjoyed greeting the local politicians and giving a gentle chiding to his favorite wait staff. To finish off the evening, Bill loved to spin a tale about the local folk or one of his World War II escapades. Billy, as Eleanor affectionately called him, was a man of integrity. By his very actions, he served as a great example to me—a mentor to be long remembered.

Through their friendship, we were repeatedly reminded of 1 Corinthians 13:7. "If you love someone, you will be loyal to him no matter what the cost. You will always believe in him, always expect the best of him and always stand your ground in defending him" (TLB). It did not matter what the circumstance—Bill and Eleanor believed in us. The differences in our ages and social status did not seem to matter. They stood by us with open arms of love and slice after slice of that scrumptious pecan pie ala mode!

When it was time for us to leave Florida for a new venture, it was difficult for many reasons. Though things fell into place as never before—in large part due to Bill's wise counsel over the years—we still haven't found anything to replace Bill and Eleanor's friendship and Billy's pecan pie.

ACTION STEP

HONESTLY EVALUATE YOUR LIFE RIGHT NOW AND IDENTIFY ONE AREA WHERE YOU WOULD LIKE TO GROW, WHERE YOU NEED SOME EXTRA GROOMING. WRITE THAT DOWN ON AN INDEX CARD. NOW LIST SEVERAL NAMES OF MEN WHO HAVE SOMETHING TO TEACH YOU IN THIS AREA. PRAY FOR THESE MEN OVER THE NEXT WEEK AND ASK GOD TO LEAD YOU TO THE PERSON—WHETHER OR NOT THEY ARE ON THE LIST—WHO CAN HELP YOU GO TO THE NEXT LEVEL.

PRAYER

Dear Heavenly Father, thank You that You take an interest in Your children's growth and development as people. Please show me ways to grow and who can help me, and who I can help in return.

DEPENDING ON GOD

STRENGTH, DETERMINATION, AND SELF-RELIANCE AREN'T ENOUGH IN LIFE— WE MUST LEARN TO TRUST GOD.

Don't try to hold God's hand; let Him hold yours.
Let Him do the holding, and you the trusting.

HAMMER WILLIAM WEBB-PEPLOE

TO THINK ABOUT

- Do you truly believe that God is still at work in the world today—in your life?
- Have you ever had to sit back and watch events unfold because there was nothing you could do to help? How did it make you feel?
- How would your responses in both good and difficult times be different if you had a deeper faith in God?

LESSON FOR LIFE

PROMISES:

God will—

Perfect His strength in
your weakness
2 Corinthians 12:9

Bring joy to the humble
Isaiah 29:19

Protect the weak
Isaiah 42:3

Provide for the humble
Psalm 22:26

Sometimes You Have to Pass the Ball

BIBLE STUDY PASSAGE: PHILIPPIANS 3:3-8

*He chose what the world thinks is unimportant and what
the world looks down on and thinks is nothing in order to
destroy what the world thinks is important.*

1 CORINTHIANS 1:28

Very few men have made a bigger splash in their chosen
profession than Michael Jordan.   He entered in the NBA in
1984 and averaged 28.4 points as a rookie.   He led the league
in scoring four of his first six seasons—but lacked what he
wanted most, a championship.   Interestingly, when he began
scoring fewer points and depending more on others, he finally
got what he coveted.

In life, we want to be masters of our destiny and our every
situation.   But too often we discover the reality that not all of
life is under our control.   A child's illness.   Company problems.
A downturn in the stock market.   Conflict among neighbors.

The good news is that with trust in God we are never
powerless or helpless.   The Apostle Paul was a formidable character: He had his day's equivalent of two doctoral degrees (law

and theology); he was a religious zealot who followed the letter of the law to a "t" (Philippians 3:6); he came from a wealthy and influential family (Philippians 3:5). But it was when he discovered that all his efforts and abilities weren't enough that he truly became a powerful force for God. He helped launch the Christian faith and turn the world upside down.

That's why he was quick to say, "The less I have, the more I depend on Him" (2 Corinthians 12:10). That's why this great orator would point out, "My teaching and preaching were not with words of human wisdom that persuade people but with proof of the power that the Spirit gives" (1 Corinthians 2:4).

God has blessed you with gifts and talents to make a difference in your world. But He's also created you with the need to depend on Him consistently.

Sometimes the greatest challenge in our lives is to not try harder but to trust more.

I cry out to God Most High, to the God who does everything for me. Psalm 57:2

REAL LIFE

Some Things Only God Can Do

ALBERT JOHNSON AS TOLD TO JENNIFER JOHNSON

Sweat beaded on her forehead and rolled down her temples. She gripped the metal arms raised on each side of the bed. Her knuckles turned white, and her face scrunched in agony. I'd never seen a person in such pain.

But she wasn't just any person.

She was my wife. I had contributed to her pain, and I couldn't help her.

Her body relaxed as the contraction subsided. "Are you okay, Jen?" I patted her arm.

She shooed my hand. "I'm fine." Looking up at me, she grinned feebly, "It's okay, Al."

Jennifer inhaled. I looked at the monitor. Another contraction was coming. I grabbed the wet washcloth from the table and wiped her brow. She shook her head and shooed me away again. "Don't touch."

Don't touch? Don't touch! My heart broke with each tear that streamed down her cheeks and each moan that escaped her lips, and she didn't want me to touch her! I had to. After all, I was the man. I could open the peanut butter jar. I could unclog faucets and toilets. I could build a whole deck in a day— okay, maybe a couple of days. It was my job to take on a task and fix it. I had to do something. I grabbed her hand, and she squeezed with brute force.

When the contraction subsided, the doctor came in and pulled back the sheet to examine her. "I think we're ready."

With those words, activity spun around us. Two nurses rearranged Jennifer on the bed and brought in supplies. Another contraction hit. Jennifer moaned and two new tears emerged.

That was it. I couldn't take anymore. Nausea welled inside me. My head felt light, and blackness closed around me. Someone was talking. "Mr. Johnson, sit down." Several shadows gathered, and I was pushed into the chair. "Sit down," that same someone said again. "Quick, get some Sprite and crackers." Within moments a cracker was shoved in my mouth, and I was sipping on Sprite.

Soon, my head started to feel normal again. I glanced at my wife. She stared at me in disbelief. Jennifer didn't understand. How could she? I'm the man, a big man, a man's man. At over two hundred pounds and well over six feet, I'm an intimidating man. I'm strong; nothing breaks me—except seeing my wife in excruciating agony.

I couldn't help her. I had to stand beside her. Hold her hand. And watch. I couldn't help.

A few hours later as I held my baby girl in my arms, I realized with overwhelming humility that there were times I couldn't fix things. Sometimes I'll have to give support, hold a hand, and watch.

Leaning over to my wife, I kissed her forehead and whispered, "I'm so proud of you." I looked at my little girl. Some things only God can do.

ACTION STEP

WHAT ARE SOME SITUATIONS YOU ARE FACING THAT YOU SIMPLY DON'T HAVE THE STRENGTH AND WISDOM TO SOLVE ON YOUR OWN? HAVE YOU SPENT TIME IN PRAYER PUTTING THESE SITUATIONS INTO GOD'S HANDS, ASKING HIM TO DO WHAT YOU ARE UNABLE TO?

WHY NOT TAKE A LONG WALK, GET AWAY FROM THE DISTRACTIONS, AND SPEND AN HOUR IN PRAYER?

PRAYER

Father, it's sometimes hard for me to admit that I can't handle some things on my own. But the truth is that I do need you—all the time, in every situation. Please be near me today.

MATERIALISM

THOUGH MONEY AND POSSESSIONS
ARE IMPORTANT, WE MUST GUARD
OUR HEARTS FROM ALLOWING THEM
TO BECOME "GODS" THAT ENSLAVE US.

*It's good to have money and the things that money can buy,
but it's good, too, to check up once in a while and make sure
that you haven't lost the things that money can't buy.*

GEORGE HORACE LORIMER

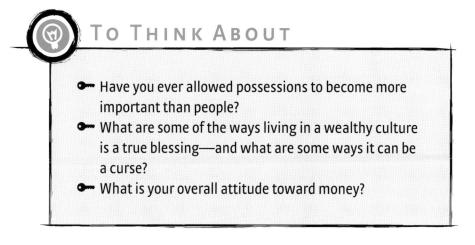

To Think About

- Have you ever allowed possessions to become more important than people?
- What are some of the ways living in a wealthy culture is a true blessing—and what are some ways it can be a curse?
- What is your overall attitude toward money?

LESSON FOR LIFE

PROMISES:

God will—

Give you true permanence and stability
1 John 2:17

Never leave you
Hebrews 13:5

Bless you beyond your expectations
Ephesians 1:3
Psalm 84:11

Priceless

BIBLE STUDY PASSAGE: MATTHEW 6:25-34

The thing you should want most is God's kingdom and doing what God wants. Then all these other things you need will be given to you.

MATTHEW 6:33

A young man came to visit Jesus and asked what he must do to become one of Jesus' followers. Jesus told the man that he must give away all his possessions and join him in his ministry right now. The young man wanted to be a disciple, but he was very rich and liked his wealth, so he sadly walked away (Matthew 19:22). No matter how much money he held onto, he was still the big loser. Because following Jesus is priceless.

To become a true disciple, do all of us need to give away our possessions and be poor? Do you? The answer is simple. If Jesus asks you to give everything, do it. If He doesn't, don't! But be aware that all of us are required to make Jesus the first priority in our lives. He must be more important than possessions. As He said to His disciples: "The thing you should want most is God's kingdom and doing what God wants. Then all these other things you need will be given to you" (Matthew 6:33).

Some of the problems that occur when we make money and things the highest values in our lives include—

- *We begin to drift away from God because of distractions.*
- *We lose a passion to serve God because we become selfish.*
- *We don't love others the same way because of greed and envy.*
- *We become unhappy and ungrateful because we focus on what we don't have instead of what we do have.*

Is it wrong to drive a nice car with the latest engineering? Is it wrong to spend a lot of money on your wardrobe? Is it wrong to buy the largest TV at the electronics store? Is it wrong to go out to eat at nice places?

The answers are between you and God. You'll want to be sure that you don't depend too much on money—as Alexandre Dumas said, "Do not value money for any more nor any less than its worth; it is a good servant but a bad master." What matters most for your soul is that you love God first and others second.

Why spend your money on something that is not real food? Why work for something that doesn't really satisfy you? Listen closely to me, and you will eat what is good; your soul will enjoy the rich food that satisfies.
Isaiah 55:2

REAL LIFE

Living My Dream

CLAY MCGUIRE AS TOLD TO ELAINE YOUNG MCGUIRE

"Mom, may my friends and I come home to wait out the hurricane?" I already knew her answer, because my friends had always been welcomed. I was less sure about my parents' response to the next request, "And may we bring the three dogs and Meghan's cat?"

After serving in Desert Storm, I studied massage therapy and rapidly moved from giving massages in a spa to managing a spa in an exclusive resort. I had always enjoyed living simply, but something changed me. Maybe it was because of my work with local celebrities, film stars, and other wealthy clientele, but soon I began buying expensive cars and lots of other "stuff."

Twice-a-year vacations to Florida turned into longing, and I decided, "I'm going to move there and live my dream." After I quit my job, I felt God blessed the decision, because I quickly landed an even better job, at an even bigger resort, and bought a beautiful house, which I filled with just-perfect furnishings.

Within a year, I sold the house and moved into a rental condominium while my newer, larger house was being built. I never totally unpacked and didn't bother with purchasing renter's insurance, since my thoughts were consumed with building decisions and plans to furnish the new house.

During the summer, my parents visited me in Pensacola, and I remember asking, "Do you want to see the house?" even before they unpacked. Although it was nearly dark, I pointed out the cherry cabinets, stainless-steel appliances, and granite countertops.

Later that week, I showed them the historic district and the beautiful towers of the resort where I worked, right on Pensacola Beach. Then we drove down miles of the protected habitat of Navarre Beach, and I beamed, "Can you believe I see this every day?"

With Hurricane Ivan's approach, my dreams turned into nightmares. Mom and Dad welcomed my friends and me, pets and all, and we watched in disbelief as the storm headed straight toward Pensacola.

We stayed on cell phones constantly: "Did you evacuate? Where are you? Are you okay?" We became frantic after one friend yelled, "I gotta go, call you back!"—then didn't. Meghan cuddled her cat, anxiety growing when she couldn't reach her husband, who'd had to remain behind, for two long days.

After learning that our Florida friends were safe, we began an Internet search to discover the fate of our homes. I was horrified to find a picture of my condominium, just a pile of rubble.

The hurricane stole all my possessions and then my job. I was blessed to quickly secure excellent employment back in Atlanta where I now live, very simply, in a small apartment furnished by people who cared.

At first I thought I'd lost everything, but, after a few days, I reflected on what had been most important while the storm raged. Then I realized that I have everything I really need: my God, family, friends, and pets who love me, and enough food, clothing, and shelter for today.

ACTION STEP

GO THROUGH YOUR CLOSET OR GARAGE AND PULL OUT EVERYTHING YOU HAVEN'T USED IN THE PAST YEAR. PRAYERFULLY FIND A WAY TO PUT THOSE THINGS IN THE HANDS OF PEOPLE WHO NEED THEM MORE THAN YOU DO— SELL CLOTHES OR BOOKS ON EBAY OR AT A GARAGE SALE AND DONATE THE MONEY TO A WORTHY MISSION IN YOUR AREA. DONATE OLD SPORTS EQUIP- MENT TO A NONPROFIT YOUTH SPORTS LEAGUE, OR OLD TOOLS TO A MISSION THAT OFFERS CAREER TRAINING. AS SOON AS YOU'RE DONE, PRAY A PRAYER OF THANKS TO GOD FOR BLESSING YOU SO ABUNDANTLY.

PRAYER

Father, I know that You love me and want good things for me. Help me put my trust in You, not in what I have.

COMMUNICATION

GREAT COMMUNICATION IS MORE THAN TECHNIQUE, BUT RATHER A REFLECTION OF HOW WE ESTEEM AND CARE FOR OTHERS.

Communication means a sharing together of what you really are. With the stethoscope of love you listen till you hear the heartbeat of the other.

BARTLETT AND MARGARET HESS

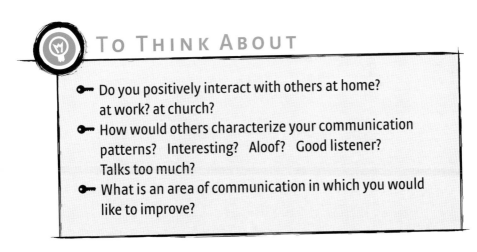

To Think About

- Do you positively interact with others at home? at work? at church?
- How would others characterize your communication patterns? Interesting? Aloof? Good listener? Talks too much?
- What is an area of communication in which you would like to improve?

LESSON FOR LIFE

PROMISES:

God will—

Provide wisdom
Proverbs 1:23

Listen to you
Psalm 4:3

Grant you love and peace
2 Corinthians 13:11

Watching Our Words Is Hard Work

BIBLE STUDY PASSAGE: PHILIPPIANS 2:5-16

When you do things, do not let selfishness or pride be your guide. Instead, be humble and give more honor to others than to yourselves.

PHILIPPIANS 2:3

We are admonished throughout all of Scripture to choose our words carefully—

- *We are to offer God praise and thanksgiving (Psalm 100:4).*
- *We are to treat the name of God with utmost respect (Exodus 20:7).*
- *We are to be gentle in the face of anger (Proverbs 15:1).*
- *We are to build others up (Ephesians 4:29).*
- *We are to avoid profanity and coarse language (Ephesians 5:4).*
- *We are to tell the truth (Exodus 20:16 and 23:1).*

The Apostle James says that our words are like the rudder on a ship or a spark that starts a forest fire—they can do great works or cause great damage (3:2-8)!

One other crucial way we are to watch our words is by

simply remaining silent and listening to others: "My dear friends, you should be quick to listen and slow to speak or to get angry" (James 1:19). If you stop to think about it, listening is actually one of the most powerful expressions of love. Because listening says to a person: *You are important to me; your ideas and feelings matter to me; share your life with me.*

We live in a fast-paced, busy, and noisy culture. The TV and radio and other forms of entertainment bombard us from morning to night. Media superstars are referred to as "talking heads." No wonder so many of us feel unheard and underappreciated. Maybe there's no one there to listen to you right now, but you could be there to listen to someone else.

In Philippians 2:4, Paul says to us: "Let each of you look out not only for his own interests, but also for the interests of others" (NKJV). The ratio of how much we listen to how much we talk is a pretty good barometer of how much we really look to the interests of others.

Does this mean that you are to be doomed to a life of never sharing what's on your heart and mind? Absolutely not! For in the same way that when we give, we receive back so much more; when we give the gift of a listening ear, others reach out in their hearts to know our souls better.

My dear brothers and sisters, always be willing to listen and slow to speak. Do not become angry easily.
James 1:19

REAL LIFE

Loud and Clear

JAY COOKINGHAM

She is sitting across the table from her husband, visibly upset with him. The tears are only the surface indicator of the stress she has been under. During the past few days, she has shared her concerns about several family matters and, although they talked about them in detail, she felt unheard. The husband is not exactly calm himself—he feels confused and hurt about such an accusation. After all, he energetically took part in the discussion. He had come up with what he thought to be a plan of action based on Scripture and faith in God's provision—what could be missing?

Then my wife said, "I don't what you to fix me; I want you to hear me." That's when I realized I was wrong, and not fully engaged in looking to my wife's interests. In the book of James, the author writes, "Always be willing to listen and slow to speak" (1:19). I had been too quick to speak, too impressed with my ability to size up the problem and pronounce a fix for it. I needed to adjust the empathy setting on the listening units on either side of my face—quickly.

My wife went on to tell me, "I want you to understand how I feel. Even if you feel what I am saying is incredibly wrong or mixed up, I need you to be patient and listen. Even if what I am saying makes you angry, I want you to think about what you are hearing, not about what you are going to say in return afterward."

Thankfully, I got the message, and we were able to connect and fully understand each other on the matter at hand. However, if I hadn't humbled myself and aimed to listen to my love's heart, we would not have been as successful in dealing with the problem. After listening intently, I knew how to pray for her concerns more effectively. More importantly, I now knew that I needed to repent, ask forgiveness, and make it a practice to really listen.

My wife has said to me that when I take this trip with her heart, she feels like I know her more deeply. She's right. Knowing that I value her thoughts creates a safe, comfortable place for openness and intimacy to flourish—she's able to talk to me more freely, which in turn grows a deeper trust between us. And I end up helping her more than I did when I just tried to "fix" the surface problem.

What a great treat: I can help empower my partner to grow in all areas of her life by simply being quick to hear, slow to speak, and slow to anger. I'm still learning—God is teaching me more every day about this wonderful woman I married. As I listen to His heart and honor His desire for His children to be good listeners, I'll be able to listen to hers in the way she needs most.

ACTION STEP

ON A SHEET OF PAPER, MAKE A CHART WITH THREE COLUMNS:

- WHO I TALKED WITH
- PERCENTAGE THEY TALKED
- PERCENTAGE I TALKED

KEEP A LOG OVER THE NEXT FEW DAYS, EVALUATING EACH CONVERSATION YOU HAVE. THEN LOOK AT YOUR CHART—DO YOU SEEM TO BE A BETTER TALKER OR A BETTER LISTENER? DO YOU THINK YOU'VE BEEN TRULY "QUICK TO LISTEN AND SLOW TO SPEAK"? WHAT SITUATIONS SEEM TO TEMPT YOU TO DOMINATE A CONVERSATION? ASK GOD TO HELP YOU IMPROVE YOUR ABILITY TO PUT OTHERS' NEEDS FIRST BY LISTENING TO THEM.

PRAYER

Father God, help me remember that people matter to You, and that their concerns should matter to me. Please make me a more patient listener.

LOSS

FAITH DOES NOT SHIELD US FROM PAIN,
BUT IT DOES PROVIDE THE WAY FOR US TO
OVERCOME EVEN THE GREATEST OF LOSS.

*In the night of death, hope sees a star,
and listening love can hear the rustle of a wing.*

ROBERT INGERSOLL

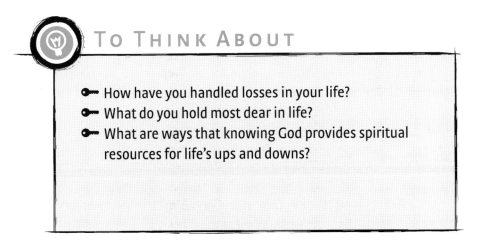

TO THINK ABOUT

- How have you handled losses in your life?
- What do you hold most dear in life?
- What are ways that knowing God provides spiritual resources for life's ups and downs?

LESSON FOR LIFE

PROMISES:

God will—

Help those who
are burdened
Psalm 145:14
Psalm 55:2

Be with you during
hard times
Isaiah 43:2

Bring you joy during grief
Psalm 30:11-12

Give you peace
Psalm 29:11

Comforted Comforters

BIBLE STUDY PASSAGE: 2 CORINTHIANS 1:2-7

He heals the brokenhearted and bandages their wounds.

PSALM 147:3

Though some misconceptions about our masculine identity try to suppress our need to face and embrace sorrow, grief is assuredly a part of life. Death. Pain. Loss. Separation. If we care about and love someone or something in a way that creates joy, then that same care and love for the person can be turned to sorrow in the face of loss.

Though we can talk about certain stages of grief—denial, anger, bargaining, depression, acceptance (first presented by Elizabeth Kubler-Ross in the book *On Death and Dying*)—there is no set timetable or "cure" for grief. The stages can occur in any variety of sequence, and certain stages may recur and dominate what we are feeling.

The good news is that the God of "all comfort" meets us right where we are. He doesn't ignore our tears, grow impatient with our questions, or condemn us for feelings of anger. He doesn't demand that we "get over it and move on" at some proscribed time. But He does embrace us and cry with us and nurse us back to health and wholeness. God knows the hurt of rejection and the horror of losing His only begotten Son on a cruel cross.

And the comfort He gives to us enables us to comfort others (2 Corinthians 1:4). It doesn't mean we are suddenly wiser and have more words to share—sometimes all a person who is grieving wants is your presence and a shoulder to cry on.

We may never understand why suffering occurs, but we can receive the tender love and compassion of God. And we can hold to the promise of a heavenly home where there are no more tears and sorrow (Revelation 21:4).

You have recorded my troubles. You have kept a list of my tears. Aren't they in your records?
Psalm 56:8

REAL LIFE

By the Grace of God

MAX DAVIS

I was going through some struggles when my friend Jimmy's wife died. Nothing in my life could have ever taught me more about God's grace during heartbreak than watching Jimmy grieve and pick up the pieces of his family.

Jimmy came home from work one day to find an ambulance in his front yard. Upon entering the house, he was shocked to find paramedics doing CPR on his thirty-one-year-old, seemingly normal, healthy, and athletic wife, Roxanne.

As Jimmy raced to the hospital in the ambulance, he was thinking, *What is happening?* He kept saying over and over, "God is faithful. God is faithful." About thirty minutes after they arrived at the hospital, the doctor led Jimmy and a few friends into a small room and said, "Roxanne suffered an aneurysm. There was nothing I could do. She's gone."

After he walked back to where Roxanne lay, Jimmy looked at her lifeless body and was overwhelmed with disbelief. Later, after leaving the hospital, he cried out, "Why, God? Roxanne was so young and beautiful. And the boys..."

As weeks went by, Jimmy struggled in deep despair—as anyone would. He saw Roxanne's clothes hanging in the closet, but he was too grief-stricken to deal with them. Finally, he asked a friend to take her clothes and donate them to charity, because he couldn't do it.

As weeks turned into months, the initial shock was replaced with deep loneliness. But through the strength of friends, his parents, and other people in the Body of Christ, Jimmy was able to continue on. He was also sustained by the Word of God, especially 2 Corinthians 12:9, where God assured Paul, "My grace is enough for you. When you are weak, my power is made perfect in you." Jimmy told me, "I've found that in my weakness, Christ would come to me."

He later said that Scripture becomes "all sustaining when we realize that God's power is sufficient. If we had not been asked to walk through the darkness of night, we would not know the sufficiency and depth of His grace. Many times through the years I've felt God's silence and I've wondered what purpose it serves. God has put within our lives pain to remind us of our dependency upon Him and scars to always recognize that I am dependent upon Him."

Fourteen years after his wife's death, through tears and many questions, his faith is stronger than ever. Jimmy has looked his opponent square in the eyes and has not run. Yes, he has experienced great grief. Sorrow and temptation he knows well. He's felt the noose of discouragement pulled tightly around his neck. And he absorbs the blows of loneliness. But Jimmy is winning by the power of Christ. God's grace and strength have become his closest allies.

When I ache over my own heartaches and weep over personal tragedies around me, I remember Jimmy. I remember seeing God pull him through and sustain him by His grace. And I press on.

ACTION STEP

IN GENESIS 22:1-14, WE READ THE POIGNANT STORY OF HOW ABRAHAM WAS WILLING TO SACRIFICE BACK TO GOD WHAT HE MOST CHERISHED. HIS LOVE FOR GOD WAS THAT GREAT. AND GOD'S LOVE FOR ABRAHAM WAS SUCH THAT HE GAVE BACK TO ABRAHAM HIS HEART'S DESIRE. WHAT DO YOU DESIRE MOST IN LIFE? HAVE YOU EVER EXPRESSED TO GOD THAT YOU LOVE HIM SO MUCH THAT HE COMES BEFORE ALL ELSE? FIND A WAY TO EXPRESS THAT TODAY. IF THE FEELINGS AREN'T THERE—IF YOU'RE HAVING TROUBLE HONESTLY SAYING TO GOD THAT YOU WOULD LOVE HIM EVEN IF THE MOST PRECIOUS THING IN YOUR LIFE WAS TAKEN AWAY—EXPRESS TO GOD THAT YOU WANT TO REACH THAT LEVEL OF LOVE FOR AND TRUST IN HIM.

PRAYER

Father God, thank You for the strength and grace You give to face hard times. Lord, today I give You my life and choose to trust You no matter what happens.

INTEGRITY IN THE WORKPLACE

THE TEMPTATION TO CHEAT IN BUSINESS
IS BOTH FIERCE AND SEDUCTIVE, BUT WILL
SHIPWRECK YOUR SOUL—AND YOUR
CAREER—IF YOU SUCCUMB.

If you have integrity, nothing else matters.
If you don't have integrity, nothing else matters.

ALAN SIMPSON

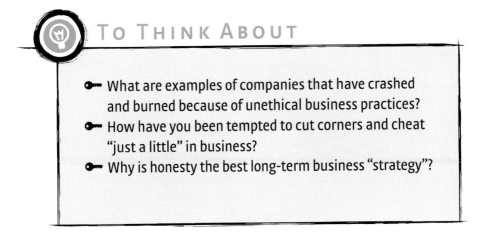

TO THINK ABOUT

- ✎ What are examples of companies that have crashed and burned because of unethical business practices?
- ✎ How have you been tempted to cut corners and cheat "just a little" in business?
- ✎ Why is honesty the best long-term business "strategy"?

LESSON FOR LIFE

PROMISES:

God will—

Perfect your character
James 1:4

Reward your honest
efforts
Job 34:11

Cause you to shine
Philippians 2:15

Bring peace to the
honest
Psalm 37:37

A Clear Conscience

BIBLE STUDY PASSAGE: PSALM 24:1-6

You must have true and honest weights and measures so that you will live a long time in the land the Lord your God is giving you.

DEUTERONOMY 25:15

One of the great needs in the workplace today is leaders with integrity. There are too many examples of the devastating impact of corporate and individual dishonesty to ignore this as a huge life issue. So what does the Bible say about integrity?

- *Integrity means treating people fairly and honestly—"The Lord wants honest balances and scales" (Proverbs 16:11). Any gain from cheating a customer or colleague is sure to be temporary. The long-term impact is always a breech of trust.*
- *Integrity is giving your word and keeping it—"Don't say things that are false" (Proverbs 24:28). Many of us want to "please" our bosses or our customers and are tempted to say what they want to hear—only to have to backtrack and apologize later. Be direct and honest up front.*

- *Integrity is more valuable than riches*—"Riches gotten by doing wrong have no value, but right living will save you from death" (Proverbs 10:2). Billions of dollars have been made—and lost—through irregular accounting practices. Thousands of lives and even communities have been destroyed by such unethical practices. True wealth comes from a true character.

- *Beware of bad influences*—"Bad friends will ruin good habits" (1 Corinthians 15:33). Just because others are cheating gives you no license to become a cheater yourself. If you work in a culture of dishonesty, address it, and if that doesn't work, move on to protect your own reputation and soul.

- *Your integrity sets an example*—"In every way be an example of doing good deeds" (Titus 2:7). Show those around you that integrity is always the best policy!

- *Integrity will be rewarded*—"Because I am innocent, you support me and will let me be with you forever" (Psalm 41:12). You may not get promoted immediately for being a man of integrity, but you will be rewarded in countless ways.

- *The Lord hates lack of integrity*—"Do not make plans to hurt your neighbors, and don't love false promises. I hate all these things" (Zechariah 8:16-17). Bottom line, we have been put on earth to praise and glorify God.

The Lord wants honest balances and scales; all the weights are his work.
Proverbs 16:11

REAL LIFE

Integrity's Reward

EDWARD SCOTT (NAME HAS BEEN CHANGED) AS TOLD TO ESTHER M. BAILEY

As a distributor representing various brands of tools, I operated our company on the principle of giving the customer a good deal for the money. That was the only way I could live with my conscience.

On standard tools from the factories, of course, buyers needed only check the published price list to verify that the appropriate discount had been given.

In addition to supplying ninety-nine lines of standard tools to the automobile plants, I also often received requests to quote on special tools. In many cases, a standard tool could be altered to required specifications. I worked with several local tool shops to have the alterations made.

Because I purchased the basic tool at the distributor's cost, I had an edge over others who quoted. Most of the time it was easy to outbid the competitors, but I made it a rule to maintain a proper balance between making a profit and serving the customer.

With my engineering background, I was sometimes asked to design a tool to be used on an assembly line for a special purpose. On those jobs I had no competition. No one else even had the specifications, so I could name my price.

The nature of my business meant that I very often had no accountability—when I was working with a tool that no one else sold, no one was checking on me to see if I was inflating the price. Especially when there was no one to keep me accountable, I made a commitment to keep myself in line. If I was tempted to take advantage of an opportunity to earn extra profit, I honored my commitment.

As a way of building trust between the customer and me, I often told buyers, "I will be happy to justify any price I quote. Just stop by the office any time and I'll show you the invoices from my suppliers." No one ever followed through on my suggestion, but the offer was always open.

One day I had lunch with the buyer at central purchasing of one of the Big Three auto companies. Hoping for heroic status within the corporation, the buyer was tough on suppliers. His motto was, "Cut costs, cut costs, cut costs."

During the course of conversation, I extended my usual offer to show him invoices to substantiate any price I quoted. A brief lull in the conversation followed as he studied my face. I thought he might be the only buyer to take me up on my offer.

He did not ask to verify prices. A short while later, he awarded our company with what was called a small value blanket order, which allowed the plants to order any item under fifty dollars without going through central purchasing.

I've been retired for several years now, but I still like to think of that special blanket order as integrity's reward.

Of course I realize that integrity does not always bring monetary gain. Sometimes it brings financial reverses or even persecution, but an even greater reward awaits those who hear Christ say, "Well done, good and faithful servant" (Matthew 25:21).

ACTION STEP

IS THERE PRESSURE IN YOUR WORKPLACE TO CUT CORNERS AND "FUDGE" JUST A LITTLE WITH YOUR WORD? YOUR INTEGRITY?

MOST COMPANIES HAVE A SET OF CORPORATE VALUES. DO YOU HAVE A PERSONAL SET OF VALUES—THAT WILL GUIDE YOU WHEN THE PRESSURE IS ON?

BEGIN NOW TO WORK ON A PERSONAL VALUE STATEMENT THAT DECLARES WHAT CAN'T BE COMPROMISED IN YOUR LIFE.

WHEN FINISHED, PUT IT ON AN INDEX CARD, HAVE IT LAMINATED, AND KEEP IT IN YOUR WALLET FOR EASY REFERENCE.

PRAYER

O God, You demand integrity because You are good and righteous—thank You for Your goodness. Lord, please continue to perfect my character and make me a man of complete integrity.

ANGER MANAGEMENT

UNCHECKED ANGER IS TOXIC FOR YOUR RELATIONSHIPS, YOUR REPUTATION, YOUR HEALTH, AND YOUR SOUL.

Anger is a killing thing: it kills the man who angers, for each rage leaves him less than he had been before—it takes something from him.

LOUIS L'AMOUR

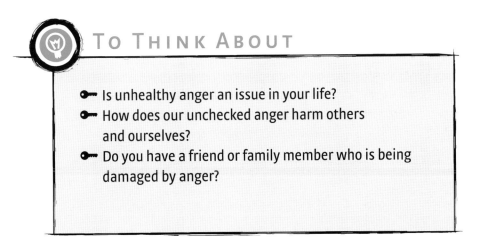

TO THINK ABOUT

- ☞ Is unhealthy anger an issue in your life?
- ☞ How does our unchecked anger harm others and ourselves?
- ☞ Do you have a friend or family member who is being damaged by anger?

LESSON FOR LIFE

PROMISES:

God will—

Grant you the fruit of
the Spirit
Galatians 5:22-23

Be patient with you
Psalm 103:8

Heal and comfort you
Isaiah 57:8

Deliver you from
harmful emotions
Psalm 147:3

Destructive Anger

BIBLE STUDY PASSAGE:

"Be angry, and do not sin": do not let the sun go down on your wrath, nor give place to the devil.

EPHESIANS 4:26

Not all anger is wrong. For one thing, God made us with emotions, and we can't just bottle up our feelings—even anger. But one crucial soul matter for many men is properly expressing and channeling anger. If your anger regularly spills over into various areas of your life, by all means get help. Why?

- *Anger is a social epidemic—from "road rage" to kicking the dog to belittling and berating children, anger is all too commonplace.*
- *Anger is physically toxic—high blood pressure, stress, and other results of anger hurt your health.*
- *Anger is toxic to relationships—anger increases hostility, decreasing peace, love, and trust.*

So how do you deal with destructive anger?

- Confession: "If we confess our sins, he will forgive our sins" (1 John 1:9). Stop making excuses. Call your unhealthy anger what it is: sinfulness against God, others, and yourself. We've all had bad days, but it's time to quit taking it out on others.
- Seek healing: "Lord, heal me, and I will truly be healed. Anger can be a manifestation of fear, anxiety, insecurity, or a deep sense of loss. No, these things don't excuse toxic behavior, but they do need to be addressed head on. Seek out a trusted Christian counselor if your anger issues are severe. But at all times, commit your past, present, and future hurts to the Great Physician.
- Replace angry habits: "If anyone belongs to Christ, there is a new creation. The old things have gone; everything is made new!" (2 Corinthians 5:17). If you curse and gripe every time you're in a traffic jam, start keeping new kinds of music in the car. If you're over competitive, put yourself on the bench.
- Starve sources of anger: "Pursue peace...lest any root of bitterness springing up cause trouble" (Hebrews 12:14-15 NKJV). Attack the root of bitterness with the incredible power of forgiveness.
- Don't give up: "So let us run the race that is before us and never give up" (Hebrews 12:1). For some of us, anger will be a lifelong battle. Yes, we will control it with God's help, but we will always feel the quick surge and tug of anger close at hand. If you blow it, go back to #1 and confess before God and others your sin—and move on.

Cease from anger, and forsake wrath; do not fret—it only causes harm.
Psalm 37:8

REAL LIFE

Leaving My Anger Behind

LARRY KARR AS TOLD TO LAROSE KARR

I can't really remember life without anger. As a boy, when my brother did things to irritate me, I just ran him through a hedge, easy then because I was bigger than him. Once I'd picked up my brother and run him through a prickly bush, I wasn't mad anymore.

Later in life, though, I couldn't seem to stop the anger. It became apparent at work when I began throwing temper tantrums. My co-workers talked about it, and I knew they had plenty to say. But they were the ones with the problem. Not me.

And then, my wife started talking to me about it. Previously she had gone into a shell and just wanted to be away from me. I guess it hit home when she wouldn't come home on her lunch hours. I knew she didn't want to deal with my problem.

One day at work in the oilfield, not long after I was saved, I was convicted to apologize to the men at work. About time for shift change, I caught the night crew coming on and the day crew leaving. I asked them to gather in the doghouse.

They thought I was going to ask to borrow money. That was the only reason they could think that I wanted them all together at the same time. Once the men assembled, I apologized for the rude behavior I exhibited toward them when angry. I asked them to forgive me and they said they would.

I wish I could say the story neatly ended there, but I can't. Several more years passed while I still struggled with anger. Our pastor came to see me one night at my wife's prompting, and we talked. You see, he knew that in a man's life when there is a deep-seated anger problem, there is a root cause.

I was able to talk to him and my wife about some childhood trauma and she in turn helped me by listening and understanding. My self-control grew by leaps and bounds, but even though I knew the root cause and had compassionate people in my life, I still blew up occasionally.

In fact, things got worse again when, at the advice of our family doctor, my wife began to stand up to me and vocalize her feelings. It just wasn't healthy for her to live in a state of fear. My final wake-up call came when she gave me an ultimatum: change or divorce. I could no longer intimidate with my size.

Solomon, the wisest man in the Bible, wrote in Proverbs 16:32: "He who is slow to anger is better than the mighty, and he who rules his spirit than he who takes a city."

Overcoming anger took a large portion of my adult life. I don't wish the battle on anyone. And believe me, it is assuredly a battle. But don't give up on yourself. As I worked through the childhood memories, angry spells, and depression, my wife and I moved into a different place in our marriage and now have a much deeper relationship as man and wife. And, praise God, we now have a life together without anger.

ACTION STEP

ANGER CAN BURST FORTH LIKE A FLASH OF LIGHTNING. BE READY TO
INSTANTLY DEAL WITH ANGER IN YOUR LIFE BEFORE IT HAS OPPORTUNITY TO
WREAK HAVOC. HERE ARE THREE VERSES TO MEMORIZE. EVERY TIME YOU
FEEL TEMPTED TO LASH OUT IN RAGE, QUOTE ONE OR ALL THREE OUT LOUD AS
A PRAYER BEFORE GOD.

- *Create in me a pure heart, God, and make my spirit right
  again* (PSALM 51:10).
- *Guide my steps as you promised; don't let any sin
  control me* (PSALM 119:133).
- *My God, I want to do what you want. Your teachings are
  in my heart* (Psalm 40:8).

PRAYER

*Father God, today I ask You for grace—I pray that I would never again hurt
someone in my anger. Thank You for Your patience and for continuing to
work in me.*

GOD'S GRACE

THOUGH GOD HAS MADE US TO BE STRONG AND RESPONSIBLE, THE FOUNDATIONAL ISSUES OF FORGIVENESS AND SALVATION ARE HIS GIFT TO US.

I guess grace doesn't have to [be] logical. If it did, it wouldn't be grace.

MAX LUCADO

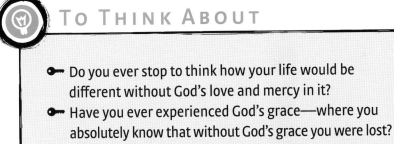

TO THINK ABOUT

- Do you ever stop to think how your life would be different without God's love and mercy in it?
- Have you ever experienced God's grace—where you absolutely know that without God's grace you were lost?
- Why is it so hard for many men to accept God's free offer of grace?

LESSON FOR LIFE

PROMISES:

God will—

Give you all good things
Psalm 84:11

Show grace and mercy
Psalm 103:8

Give grace for your time
of need
Hebrews 4:16

Provide for your needs
Leviticus 26:4-5

Riches of Grace

BIBLE STUDY PASSAGE: EPHESIANS 2:1-10

But he said to me, "My grace is enough for you. When you are weak, my power is made perfect in you." So I am very happy to brag about my weaknesses. Then Christ's power can live in me.

2 CORINTHIANS 12:9

Did you know God favors you? Not because you are the smartest; not because you are the strongest; not because you have lots of talents; not because you are so handsome; not because you do many good deeds—though all of these characteristics may be abundant in your life!

No, God favors you out of His deep, abiding love for you, a love that is not contingent upon any effort you put forth. In fact, if you declared yourself to be God's enemy today, He would love you just as much.

• God's grace is a wonderful reality that is available for you right now. Here are some aspects of grace that just might be what you need to hear today:

- *Grace means God loved you and knew you before you were even born. God said to Jeremiah: "Before I made you in your mother's womb, I chose you. Before you were born, I set you apart for a special work. I appointed you as a prophet to the nations" (Jeremiah 1:5).*
- *Grace provides the gift of salvation, a gift that can't be earned. Paul says: "You have been saved by grace through believing. You did not save yourselves; it was a gift from God" (Ephesians 2:8).*

Grace is available to us when we are weak. Paul says: "So I am very happy to brag about my weaknesses. Then Christ's power can live in me" (2 Corinthians 12:9).

- *Grace is sufficient for absolutely any need we have—whether health, finances, relationships, temptations, or any other need. Paul says: "My grace is sufficient for you" (2 Corinthians 12:9 NKJV).*
- *Grace provides us with the strength we need to overcome temptation and live a victorious Christian life. Says Peter, "Jesus has the power of God, by which he has given us everything we need to live and to serve God. We have these things because we know him" (2 Peter 1:3).*

The truth is that we are all in desperate need of God's grace. Whatever you're facing today, be assured: God is on your side. He is ready and able to help you as you respond to Him with faith.

May the Lord show you his kindness and have mercy on you.

Numbers 6:25

REAL LIFE

Jim

DAVID FLANAGAN

"Davey, can you help me?" I looked and realized that Jim, my neighbor and the father of several of my friends, was propped up against the cold, rusty stairwell on the second floor of Charlestown's Bunker Hill housing projects, legless and totally out of it.

I looked at his hair, which seemed to be desperately trying to escape from his cap, his sun-browned, wrinkled face, and tired eyes trying to focus on me. "What do you want, Jim?" I asked, with more irritation than patience. I did feel bad for him—this wasn't the first time that I had seen him roasting under a fog of alcohol, asking for some change or a little conversation.

All Jim wanted this time was a lift home—one traveled upon the shoulder of an embarrassed, shy twelve-year-old. I helped him from the stairwell.

I felt a thousand eyes upon us as we approached Carney Court. Dozens of kids were playing in the summer sun—how could I have thought our journey would go unnoticed? We stumbled along, moving much more slowly than I could bear. Please let this ordeal be over soon.

Soon I could see his son Billy—and he saw us.

My mind soaked up the look on Billy's face as his father and I drew closer to him and our friends. Billy walked over, thanked me, and without a word to his father relieved me of my burden. I walked away, embarrassed about being seen with Jim and having to deliver him to his son—my friend—in that condition. My shame could only have paled in comparison to that felt by Billy and his family.

Jim passed away several years later, but his pride, will, and his family's hopes had died long before. Jim's four sons ended up involved in violent crimes and at least two were sentenced to Walpole Prison. One is still there, having spent half his life behind bars.

I have since left the projects, married, and had children. Sometimes I look at my sons and shudder—they're so precious. What if I'd become a Jim, a burden to them? Who would they become? I can't stand to think of them in jail, their spirits broken. I can't stand the idea of missing their lives in a state of incoherence.

Jim and his family lost their battle with alcohol very publicly and tragically. And the kid who once helped Jim home has escaped alcoholism and despair. I can't take credit for that—I made some good decisions, but it was God who delivered me safely from my background, and I know I owe a huge debt of gratitude to Him. I guess all I can do to thank Him is embrace the treasures He has given me and commit to be a good steward of my wife and children.

Sometimes we learn through negative examples. Maybe that's one positive legacy of Jim's life—I know how bad things could be and that all that I am and have become is truly a gift of God's grace.

ACTION STEP

Scripture tell us that "Even though you are bad, you know how to give good gifts to your children. How much more your heavenly Father will give good things to those who ask him!" (Matthew 7:11).

Have fun with this activity. Buy a small "just because I love you" surprise gift for your children, or if you don't have children of your own, a neighbor's kid. Wrap it up and present it with a smile and a huge "I love you!"

Now reflect on how God feels about bestowing grace on you!

PRAYER

Lord, You are good and Your love endures forever. Thank You so much for my life. Help me share Your grace with others.

A GENEROUS SPIRIT

GOD CALLS US TO SHARE FROM OUR ABUNDANCE WITH THOSE IN NEED— EVEN WHEN WE FEEL NEEDY OURSELVES.

It has been well remarked, it is not said that after keeping God's commandments, but in keeping them there is great reward. God has linked these two things together, and no man can separate them—obedience and peace.

FREDERICK WILLIAM ROBERTSON

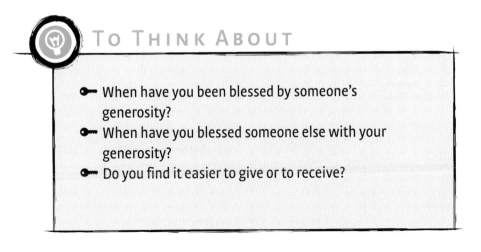

TO THINK ABOUT

- ⚷ When have you been blessed by someone's generosity?
- ⚷ When have you blessed someone else with your generosity?
- ⚷ Do you find it easier to give or to receive?

LESSON FOR LIFE

PROMISES:

God will—

Enrich your life in
all ways
Deuteronomy 30:19-20
John 10:10

Make you joyful
through giving
2 Corinthians 9:7

Bless your obedience
Psalm 119:2

Multiply your gifts
Luke 6:38

Never leave you
Hebrews 13:5

The Gift of Giving

BIBLE STUDY PASSAGE: ROMANS 12:1-10

"Bring to the storehouse a full tenth of what you earn so there will be food in my house.   Test me in this," says the Lord All-Powerful.   "I will open the windows of heaven for you and pour out all the blessings you need."

MALACHI 3:10

One of the true tests of our character is what we do with our money. Of course, God calls us to give a portion of our income to Him through ministry (Numbers 18:28) and to also give special sacrificial offerings to meet special needs as we feel directed in our hearts (Numbers 15:3). Paul does say that some people have a special gift of giving (Romans 12:8), but he also points out that God loves a cheerful giver (2 Corinthians 9:7), and Jesus himself drew attention to the meager gift of a poor widow as a true model of generosity (Matthew 12:43-44).

When we are generous, a number of healthy dynamics are fostered in our lives—

- We acknowledge that God owns everything and we have only been appointed as caretakers. The psalmist declares on behalf of God: "Every animal of the forest is already mine. The cattle on a thousand hills are mine" (Psalm 50:10).
- We clutch less tightly to what we can generate and become more aware that all good gifts come from God. James tells us: "every perfect gift is from God. These good gifts come down from the Creator of the sun, moon, and stars, who does not change like their shifting shadows" (James 1:17).
- We learn to trust and serve God with a pure heart. Jesus told his disciples: "No one can serve two masters. . . .You cannot serve both God and worldly riches" (Matthew 6:24).
- We receive the joy that comes from helping someone in need (Matthew 25:23).
- We become more confident and trusting, and begin to eliminate worry from our lives (Philippians 4:5-7, 17).
- We become better stewards in all areas of our finances. The more we give the more we seem to have (Matthew 19:29).

Whoever gives to others will get richer; those who help others will themselves be helped.

Proverbs 11:25

The most important gift that God wants you to offer Him is your very life (Romans 12:1-2). Then He can teach you that whatever we grasp, dries up and suffocates. Whatever we give freely, takes off and soars.

REAL LIFE

From Darkness to Light

JIM SNIPES AS TOLD TO NANETTE THORSEN-SNIPES

After my third job layoff in six years, I stood at the stove browning hamburger while my wife worked in her office. I stepped away to go through the bills. Before I could slide back over to the stove, Nan had rescued the burning hamburger—our last package of ground beef. In an effort to help, I'd created a disaster.

Being laid off after twenty-six years with a company was bad, but even worse were the next two layoffs and the continual loss of salary. I wondered what would become of us.

During the first layoff, I felt discouraged. I had worked hard to get into management. In twenty-six years, I'd missed less than ten days of sickness and had been a loyal employee, but learned that everyone was expendable.

One day, Nan interrupted my daily ritual of sending out résumés. "Jim," she said, "I just heard on TV that Hurricane Mitch destroyed Honduras."

What did I care? Honduras was a million miles away from thoughts of gaining employment.

She continued, "The people there have nothing. They only have the clothes on their backs."

I had to find a job, and she was getting on my nerves.

"I think we should give some food to the Hondurans," she began. "And we have some old clothes we can send, too."

I could feel the heat rising in my face. What? Give food to someone else? We could barely feed ourselves.

I began to argue, but stopped when she said she felt as if God was prompting her. Later that day we took the items to a nearby church. While standing in the basement talking to the pastor, Nan whispered that we should give more. I nodded in agreement. I pulled out our checkbook. Within minutes, I'd written a check for $100—money we could ill afford to spend.

Because of our obedience, the job doors swung open. By stepping outside of ourselves and giving sacrificially to the least of these, God began pouring out blessings, and I gained employment.

When I lost my job the third time, we faithfully read through the Psalms. Psalm 18:28-29 became my war cry: "With your help I can attack an army. With God's help I can jump over a wall."

One worry was our pre-existing health issues; we needed to be insured or risk losing our insurability. Interim insurance was costly, but we had to have it.

One day, with my spirits flagging, I opened my mailbox to find a letter from our church. "We have received an anonymous donation for you. The donor is praying for you and felt directed by God to help." Tears welled in my eyes. That check would pay for our insurance.

While my faith was challenged, I never stopped believing that "with my God I can scale a wall." Again, God faithfully provided, and two weeks after we received that check, I began my fourth job, which turned out to be the place God had for me all along.

ACTION STEP

LOOK FOR A SPECIAL NEED IN YOUR COMMUNITY, NEIGHBORHOOD, OR CHURCH. ASK GOD TO IMPRESS ON YOUR HEART WHAT YOU CAN GIVE TO BLESS THAT PERSON OR FAMILY IN THEIR SITUATION. IF AT ALL POSSIBLE, MAKE YOUR GIFT IN SECRET AND KEEP IT BETWEEN YOU AND GOD.

PRAYER

I praise You, O God, who meets all my needs and lavishes me with all kinds of blessings.   Thank You for enabling me to be generous with others.

NEW PATHS

THE ONLY THING HOLDING YOU BACK FROM EMBARKING ON NEW OPPORTUNITIES GOD PUTS ON YOUR HEART ARE YOUR OWN FEARS AND DOUBTS.

Find a job you like and you add five days to every week.

H. JACKSON BROWNE

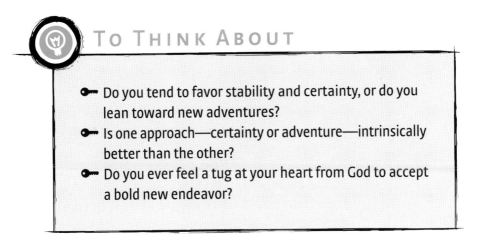

TO THINK ABOUT

- ☛ Do you tend to favor stability and certainty, or do you lean toward new adventures?
- ☛ Is one approach—certainty or adventure—intrinsically better than the other?
- ☛ Do you ever feel a tug at your heart from God to accept a bold new endeavor?

LESSON FOR LIFE

PROMISES:

God will—

Give you happiness in
His word
Psalm 119:35

Give you what you need
2 Peter 1:3

Give you peace
Matthew 11:28

Be with you
Isaiah 43:2

The Grass Is Always Greener

BIBLE STUDY PASSAGE: PSALM 23

Listen now to my voice; I will give you counsel, and God will be with you.

EXODUS 18:19 NKJV

Psalm 23 is one of the most common Bible passages recited at funerals.   But it is even more a fabulous expression of how God leads and guides us on the adventure of life.

First of all, we can trust God's guidance—even in bold, frightening new areas. David teaches us that He—

- *Provides for our physical needs—"He makes me to lie down in green pastures" (v. 2).*
- *Provides for our emotional needs—"He restores my soul" (v. 3).*
- *Provides for our spiritual needs—"He leads me in the paths of righteousness (v. 3b).*

Knowing that God provides for our needs is a wonderful comfort and resource. But David says that God is also with us in the storms that accompany a new venture. He declares that God—

- *Never leaves us "out there" on our own—"For You are with me" (v. 4).*
- *Redirects us when we need course correction—"Your rod and Your staff" (v. 4).*
- *Communes with us in times of trouble—"They comfort me" (v. 4).*

If God calls you to a new pasture, be assured He will not leave you to languish, but according to David will give you—

- *Peace—"You prepare a table before me in the presence of my enemies" (v. 5).*
- *Hope—"Surely goodness and mercy shall follow me All the days of my life" (v. 6).*
- *A sure future—"And I will dwell in the house of the Lord forever" (v. 6).*

The pundits tell us to beware that "the grass is always greener on the other side of the fence." But when God calls us to new pastures, it's true.

He makes me to lie down in green pastures; He leads me beside the still waters. He restores my soul; He leads me in the paths of righteousness for His name's sake.

Psalm 23:2-3 NKJV

REAL LIFE

Pastures of Hope

GARRETT FRYE AS TOLD TO RONDI FEYEREISEN

The pastures of my life were not green anymore. Despite the loving wife, healthy children, beautiful new home, and secure job, I felt myself slipping down a gradual slope into a land of despair and hopelessness. If something didn't change, I would not survive.

Pain. I had to get away from the pain.

At the prompting of a good friend, I sought career counseling. My job profile had changed over the last several years to the point where I felt like a square peg being jammed into a round hole. It didn't fit, and I was wearing out in the process. Eventually, this stress affected the most important areas of my life—my relationship with my wife and children became painfully strained and began to disintegrate.

I longed for greener pastures.

As part of the counselor's recommended plan, I took a graduate-level class in the area of my identified strengths at a local university. I was dipping my toe in the waters of change, feeling both excited and apprehensive as I entered the classroom. It had been twenty years. Would I be able to handle the academic challenge? And what if this proved to be the right direction for me? Would my family be willing to support my going back to school full time? After all, in the next few years, three of our children would go off to college.

How would we do it?

Answers to those questions materialized throughout the semester. Although the class was challenging, I knew it was where I belonged. So, after long talks with my wife, much counsel from friends, and a lot of prayer, we made the decision to go for it. I would leave my secure job and enter the world of academia to pursue my doctorate. It would be a long journey, over five years.

I felt my Shepherd telling me that He had greener pastures ahead for me, and I felt hope for the first time in years.

As I look back, I wish I could say that all was bliss from that point on. Yes, there was tremendous relief, but the journey involved a lot of work—restoring our marriage, healing emotionally and mentally, stretching our finances, not to mention handling the academic load. My family was supportive, but there were struggles and sacrifices along the way. Pastures don't become green again overnight. It took a while for us to trudge through the valley.

Seven years ago, I had almost given up hope. But I am no longer that man of yesterday. Physically, emotionally, intellectually, socially, and spiritually, I am restored. Christian friends were part of that process—three men in my small group who listened and prayed, a man at work who helped me confront truth, my pastor who came alongside me, my counselor who redirected my focus back to my Shepherd.

My Shepherd—who led me back to green pastures, who restored my soul, who restored my hope.

ACTION STEP

WHAT DO YOU WANT TO BE WHEN YOU GROW UP? YOU MAY BE ON THE EXACT RIGHT PATH AT THE EXACT RIGHT PLACE TODAY, BUT SOMETIMES GOD CALLS US OUTSIDE OUR COMFORT ZONES INTO NEW CAREERS, NEW MINISTRY OPPORTUNITIES, EVEN NEW LOCATIONS. IF YOU'VE FELT STIRRINGS IN YOUR HEART, WRITE DOWN A LIST OF TEN NEW WAYS YOU CAN SERVE GOD AND OTHERS. ASK GOD TO HELP YOU MOVE FORWARD TODAY!

PRAYER

Lord, thank You for being such a wonderful Shepherd. Please guide my thoughts and plans today as I seek to follow You.

GOD'S VOICE

GOD DOES NOT USUALLY SHOUT NOR FORCE US TO LISTEN, SO WE MUST MAINTAIN OPEN AND RECEPTIVE HEARTS.

God does not have to come and tell me what I must do for Him, He brings me into a relationship with Himself where I hear His call and understand what He wants me to do, and I do it out of sheer love to Him. When people say they have had a call to foreign service, or to any particular sphere of work, they mean that their relationship to God has enabled them to realize what they can do for God.

OSWALD CHAMBERS

TO THINK ABOUT

- Do you believe that God speaks directly to people today?
- Have you ever sensed God's voice in your life?
- If God wanted to get hold of you with a special task— how hard would it be to get your attention?

LESSON FOR LIFE

PROMISES:

God will—

Speak in a still,
small voice
1 Kings 19:12

Call you by name
John 10:3

Be a light on your path
Psalm 16:11
Psalm 119:105

Direct your steps
Isaiah 30:21

A Whisper in the Night

BIBLE STUDY PASSAGE: 1 SAMUEL 3:1-10

Speak, Lord.   I am your servant and I am listening.

1 SAMUEL 3:10

Sometimes as men we are accused of selective hearing—we can pick up the score for a ballgame from the radio of a car racing by at fifty miles per hour, but miss three of the items needed at the grocery store from two feet away. The same might be said in our spiritual lives. How closely do we listen for God's voice to lead and direct us?

God speaks to everyone through His Word. Everything we need to know about loving Him and others is clearly spelled out. But sometimes God speaks in special ways, under special circumstances, with a special message to us individually.

God speaks to us through—

- *Our own thoughts—if we read His Word and talk to Him in prayer, it shouldn't surprise us when we begin coming up with ideas that seem heaven-sent. "Lord, every morning you hear my voice. Every morning, I tell you what I need, and I wait for your answer" (Psalm 5:3).*

- *The thoughts of others—again, if we talk about God with others who know Him and love Him, we should expect to hear His voice in the words of a trusted friend. "A good person speaks with wisdom, and he says what is fair" (Psalm 37:30).*
- *A question or problem that won't go away—often, when we sense a special need in our community or in our own life, God is prompting us to discover something He wants us to do about it through us. We are often His answers to others' prayers. "God called Paul to Macedonia by giving him a vision of a Macedonian man begging for help" (Acts 16:9-10).*
- *A sermon or song—when we go to church with an open heart and mind, we should expect to hear a special word from God through the music and preaching. "Come, let us go up to the mountain of the Lord, to the Temple of the God of Jacob. Then God will teach us his ways, and we will obey his teachings" (Isaiah 2:3).*
- *A still, small voice—though people might think we're crazy, it's true that God does directly impress His thoughts on our minds today. Even as He called Samuel to be His prophet in the still of the night (1 Samuel 3:4), sometimes He chooses to make Himself known directly on our hearts.*

The real question is not whether God speaks today, but how well do we listen?

Then I heard the Lord's voice, saying, "Whom can I send? Who will go for us?" So I said, "Here I am. Send me!"

Isaiah 6:8

 ## REAL LIFE

Saving Jael

CURT KONECKY AS TOLD TO C. HOPE FLINCHBAUGH

We were totally caught off guard that night. Doesn't God usually do something like this under a more spiritual setting? I wondered.

That night, the show "Touched by an Angel" told a powerful story that marked the ten-year anniversary of the 1988 Tiananmen Square massacre. As interesting as the story was, I only saw the children crying on my TV screen.

Feeling almost silly, I wiped tears away with the back of my hand and looked over at my wife, Jan. Tears were streaming down her face, too.

Our two kids looked back at us with a question practically printed across their foreheads—What's going on with you guys?

Janet and I didn't say much, but that night, as we lay in bed holding hands, some thing, or some one, descended upon us like a heavy blanket. Afraid to move, I sensed the overwhelming presence of God and wondered if we were being "touched by an angel."

After some time, the "blanket" lifted and Janet asked me, "Did you hear anything?"

"You won't believe it," I answered.

"Maybe I will believe it if it's the same thing I just heard."

We were confounded when we realized that we both heard the exact same words at the exact same time: *I want you to save a life in China.*

Three days later, my wife called an adoption agency. She said, "You don't know me. But God has shown my husband and me that He wants us to save a life in China." Janet started crying. "I know this sounds really stupid."

"This is very interesting," the woman answered. "Because the last phone call I received was at midnight last night. There's a little girl in an orphanage and they called asking for help to save the life of this child in China."

The baby had hydrocephalus, a condition of water on the brain that needed to be corrected medically as soon as possible or the damage could be irreversible. Unless the adoption moved quickly, she could be brain damaged by the time we got her—and that could change our lives forever.

Our church put up a signup sheet for church members to take turns fasting and praying for our adoption process. I really feel it was prayer that in the end released our baby into our arms.

We were finally in China and the orphanage director handed us our new eighteen-month-old daughter. All the pent up emotions and desire, months of paperwork, praying on my knees, and waiting swept over me. She was in my arms and I just wept. I totally lost it.

Jael's surgeries have been successful. When we're in public, questions naturally come up. I love to tell about what God has done in getting Jael into our arms. Who knows? Maybe they will look into the face of our small Chinese child and believe that they, too, can be "touched by an angel."

ACTION STEP

JAMES SAYS OF WISDOM THAT "IF ANY OF YOU NEEDS WISDOM, YOU SHOULD ASK GOD FOR IT. HE IS GENEROUS AND ENJOYS GIVING TO ALL PEOPLE, SO HE WILL GIVE YOU WISDOM. BUT WHEN YOU ASK GOD, YOU MUST BELIEVE AND NOT DOUBT. ANYONE WHO DOUBTS IS LIKE A WAVE IN THE SEA, BLOWN UP AND DOWN BY THE WIND" (VV. 5-6). WHEN WAS THE LAST TIME YOU SPECIFI-CALLY ASKED GOD TO SPEAK TO YOU ABOUT A PARTICULAR STRUGGLE? A RELA-TIONSHIP ISSUE? YOUR FUTURE? YOUR SERVICE TO HIM AND OTHERS?

SOME MEN LIKE TO SET ASIDE A WEEKEND EACH YEAR TO HAVE A PRAYER "RETREAT"—A TIME TO BE ALONE WITH GOD IN PRAYER. MAYBE YOU AREN'T READY TO SPEND THAT AMOUNT OF TIME, BUT WHAT ABOUT ONE FULL HOUR AWAY FROM DISTRACTIONS AND CELL PHONES TO JUST PRAY? MAKE AN APPOINTMENT NOW!

PRAYER

God of the universe, I'm amazed that You speak to us so quietly and so often. Please soften my heart and give me ears to hear You today.

RAISING CHILDREN

RAISING GREAT CHILDREN IS A TREMENDOUS CHALLENGE, RESPONSIBILITY, AND JOY.

The words that a father speaks to his children in the privacy of home are not heard by the world, but, as in whispering-galleries, they are clearly heard at the end and by posterity.

JEAN PAUL RICHTER

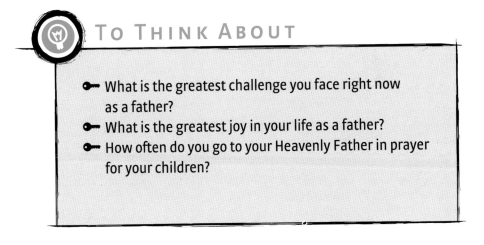

TO THINK ABOUT

- What is the greatest challenge you face right now as a father?
- What is the greatest joy in your life as a father?
- How often do you go to your Heavenly Father in prayer for your children?

LESSON FOR LIFE

PROMISES:

God will—

Crown your efforts
with success
Proverbs 16:3

Make you more
like Christ
Romans 8:29

Reveal himself to you as
you love your children
Matthew 25:21

Give you wisdom
James 1:5

Turn your kids' hearts
toward you
Malachi 4:6

Train Up a Child

BIBLE STUDY PASSAGE: DEUTERONOMY 6:19

*Train children how to live right, and when they are old,
they will not change.*

PROVERBS 22:6

After the children of Israel were delivered from slavery in
Egypt, had passed through the long, arduous journey of the wilderness, and were poised to move into the Promised Land, a great
challenge was given to the fathers that would bless not only their
own lives, but also the lives of their children and grandchildren.
Who of us as loving fathers don't want to leave that kind of legacy?

Challenge #1: Be obedient—"Obey all his rules and
commands I give you so that you will live a long time"
(Deuteronomy 6:1-2). Do you want to raise happy and obedient
children? There's no better place to begin than your own obedience. There are no shortcuts on teaching the most important
lessons in life. We have to model them.

Challenge #2: Pursue God's truth—"Listen, Israel, and carefully obey these laws. Then all will go well for you" (6:3-4). In a
society that celebrates moral relativism, we seem surprised when

our children can't distinguish between right and wrong. Do you pursue truth by honoring God and His Word?

Challenge #3: Love God—"Love the Lord your God with all your heart, all your soul, and all your strength" (6:5-6). Have you noticed that raising great kids is really about becoming the kind of person God wants us to be? Do you love God with all your heart? That is a lesson that is easier caught than taught!

Challenge #4: Teach God's Word—"Teach them to your children, and talk about them when you sit at home and walk along the road, when you lie down and when you get up" (6:7-9). In Old Testament times, parents would have a box on their doorpost that contained Bible verses to be read aloud whenever someone entered or left the house. Do you read Bible stories to your kids? Do you have verses posted in your home?

Challenge #5: Don't follow false gods—"Do not forget the Lord, who brought you out of the land of Egypt where you were slaves" (6:10-19). Even 5,000 years later, we are still faced with the temptation to follow false gods—gods of materialism and pleasure and success. Your children need to see a dad who is faithful to the one true God!

Every loving father wants to bless his children. And you can do it with time, patience, consistency, humility, and a complete trust in God.

The father of a good child is very happy; parents who have wise children are glad because of them.

Proverbs 23:24

REAL LIFE

Family Resemblance

JAY COOKINGHAM

I had just arrived home late from work and was feeling sick and bone weary. My spirit was past spent and I wanted to plop down somewhere and ignore everything and everyone. But my day wasn't through—I needed to make my "rounds," checking in with my kids and asking how their day had gone.

Sarah, my oldest daughter, had her feelings hurt at dance class earlier that afternoon, so she was first on my list. Walking into her room, I put my arms around her as she began to cry. In between sobs, she shared about how she didn't get the part in the recital that she wanted, and then another girl said something really mean...

My head was throbbing and my eyes were nearly shut by the pain, but I managed to listen closely to all the details. We discussed how to handle disappointment, and as we prayed together, she was able to release her sorrow to God.

After some prayer and "daddy" time, Sarah felt better, and I moved on to catch up with the rest of the crew. Dinnertime, story time, and then the kids' bedtime came in rapid succession. Afterwards, I went downstairs to the family room to channel surf myself numb.

For weeks I had been feeling unworthy of the adoration I saw in my children's eyes. Sitting alone, doubts about my fathering skills kept pecking at me—the same doubts about the impact I was having on their young lives that had been keeping me awake lately. I worried that I wasn't quite the hero my daughter had pictured in her mind, that I wasn't the man my sons believed me to be. As I tried to lose myself in cable land, those uncertainties kept fighting for my attention—you're not a good father and never will be. Just what kind of example are you setting? The lies kept coming, and my spirit felt worse than my throbbing head.

After a short while, my wife came in, hugged me from behind, and told me something that would lift my spirits and encourage my heart. As she was saying goodnight to my daughter, Sarah had told her, "Mom, Daddy is the one person that shows me Jesus the best."

How I needed to hear those words! They were the tonic I needed to ease the despair that was killing me. As my tears flowed, I realized that my daughter noticed that Daddy wasn't feeling well, yet took the time to listen to her heart. She saw a picture of Christ's character fleshed out in me when I was willing to pursue her despite the way I felt. The family resemblance displayed before her young eyes was that of the Heavenly Father, who enabled me to "look like Jesus" to my daughter.

ACTION STEP

YOU'VE SEEN PLENTY OF VERSE-A-DAY CALENDARS, E-MAIL NEWSLETTERS, AND BOOKS—WHY NOT MAKE YOUR OWN? CHOOSE A MONTH'S WORTH OF VERSES THAT HAVE SPECIAL MEANING TO YOU, AND PLOT THEM ON A CALENDAR. READ A VERSE EVERY NIGHT AT DINNER OR BEDTIME. START OVER AT THE END OF THE MONTH!

PRAYER

Heavenly Father, I know that You care about my kids more than I do. Help me today to point them toward you.

WAITING ON GOD

GOD'S TIMETABLE ISN'T ALWAYS THE SAME AS OURS—BUT HE ALWAYS PROVIDES WHAT WE MOST NEED WHEN WE MOST NEED IT.

*Remember you are very special to God as His precious child.
He has promised to complete the good work He has begun in you.*

GARY SMALLEY AND JOHN TRENT

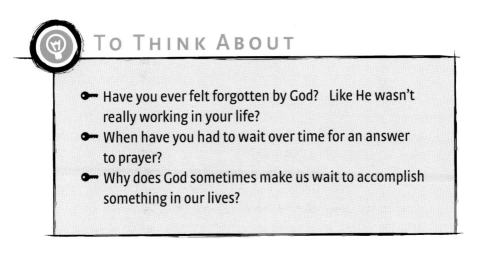

TO THINK ABOUT

- Have you ever felt forgotten by God? Like He wasn't really working in your life?
- When have you had to wait over time for an answer to prayer?
- Why does God sometimes make us wait to accomplish something in our lives?

LESSON FOR LIFE

PROMISES:

God will—

Give wisdom and
provision
Isaiah 28:29

Accomplish His plans
Proverbs 19:21

Always remember you
Nahum 1:7

Provide for all your needs
Philippians 4:19

Hold On

BIBLE STUDY PASSAGE: GENESIS 50:15-26

*You meant to hurt me, but God turned your evil into good
to save the lives of many people, which is being done.*

GENESIS 50:20

God promised to make Abraham the father of a great
nation, with descendants as numerous as the stars in the sky
(Genesis 15:5).   Despite his great faith, can you blame him for
questioning when this was going to happen when he was still
fatherless at age seventy-five (Genesis 12:4)?

Samuel anointed David as king of Israel in response to
Saul's spirit of disobedience (1 Samuel 16:1).   The problem
was that David was hunted like a fugitive and animal for the
next seven years (1 Samuel 19:9).   No wonder he cried to God,
"Why have you forgotten me? Why am I sad and troubled by my
enemies?" (Psalm 42:9).

Moses led the Hebrew slaves from captivity and into the
Promised Land—over the course of forty years (Exodus 16:35).
Jesus spent the first thirty years of His life as a child, son,
student, brother, and carpenter before the right moment came

for Him to begin His ministry (Luke 3:23).

Why doesn't God just bring about His plans in our lives right now?   Could it be that one of the most important ways God forms us into the image of His Son Jesus Christ is through allowing us to express our faith in Him through waiting?

In the Proverb, Solomon points out the natural truism that "it is sad not to get what you hoped for.   But wishes that come true are like eating fruit from the tree of life" (13:12).   But Paul's testimony that "The sufferings we have now are nothing compared to the great glory that will be shown to us" (Romans 8:18) is a powerful reminder that God may not be early—but He's always right on time with just what we need.

Is your soul weary with worry?   Are you frustrated waiting to know God wants to do in your life?   Hold on.   God is on the way right now.

Lord, you are my God. I honor you and praise you, because you have done amazing things. You have always done what you said you would do; you have done what you planned long ago. Isaiah 25:1

REAL LIFE

God Is Never Late

STAN TOLER

Several years ago, I attended a service where a friend was preaching. As we entered the sanctuary, each attendee received a brown paper lunch bag that was labeled "God Bag." In addition, white strips of paper were distributed to each person. As my friend concluded his powerful message, he asked each person in attendance to write down his or her hurts, problems, and needs and put them in the God Bag. I joined with others in making my list.

One hurt was especially painful to write down. A person whom I had employed and trusted as a friend had betrayed me. It appeared that the lie that was being told about me would never be corrected. Because it raised questions about my integrity, I was especially hurt and upset. Day after day, I had thought about the incident, often weeping bitterly in prayer, asking God to deal with my offender.

Finally, after allowing each of us time to finish writing, my friend instructed each person to prayerfully commit their concerns to the Lord and put them into the bag. And he told us to remove the strips of paper only as our prayers were answered.

With a sense of relief and childlike faith, I placed my concerns in the God Bag. I felt better immediately! (Yes, even about my offender.)

Daily I began praying the Lord's Prayer. In that prayer, Jesus taught us to pray, "Forgive us our debts as we forgive our debtors." I chose not to curse or rehearse my hurts. I cupped my hands before the Lord and symbolically gave them over to God. I then raised my hands in prayer and claimed victory over my hurts.

Time passed and with each answer to prayer, I removed a strip of paper and gave thanks to God. Five years passed, and all but one strip of paper had been removed. You guessed it—there had been no contact from my offender. Then, one Saturday evening as I sat putting the finishing touches on my Sunday morning message titled "What Is Forgiveness?" the phone rang. It was the person who had attacked my credibility.

The tearful voice said, "It's been years since I've talked to you. Will you forgive me for lying about you? Christ has forgiven me, and now I need to know—Stan, will you forgive me?" Without hesitation, I said, "You already have my forgiveness!"

What peace flooded my soul as I went to my office and took out the last strip of paper from the God Bag! God is never late in matters of forgiveness— or any other matter. He knows the very moment that our souls need relief!

ACTION STEP

SET UP A TIME TO VISIT WITH A SENIOR CITIZEN WHO HAS EXEMPLIFIED A JOYFUL AND FAITHFUL WALK WITH GOD. ASK THE PERSON TO SHARE A FEW STORIES ABOUT WHEN THEY HAD TO WAIT PATIENTLY FOR GOD TO ACT ON A SPECIAL NEED IN HIS OR HER LIFE.

PRAYER

Great is Your faithfulness, O God, my Redeemer. Thank You for being true to Your word by never leaving or forsaking me.

SERVING GOD

WE SERVE GOD WHEN WE SERVE OTHERS.

*I am a little pencil in the hand of a writing God
who is sending a love letter to the world.*

MOTHER TERESA

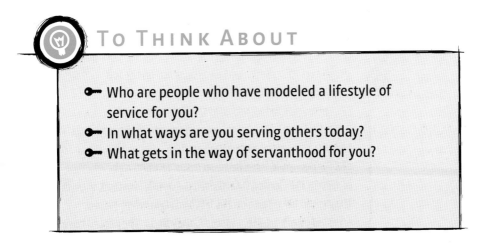

TO THINK ABOUT

- Who are people who have modeled a lifestyle of service for you?
- In what ways are you serving others today?
- What gets in the way of servanthood for you?

LESSON FOR LIFE

PROMISES:

God will—

Bless your compassion
Matthew 10:42

Appreciate your giving
2 Corinthians 9:7

Bless you and allow you to bless others
2 Corinthians 9:8

Bless you as you seek to bless others
Proverbs 11:25

The Towel and Basin Society

BIBLE STUDY PASSAGE: JOHN 13:1-20

If I then, your Lord and Teacher, have washed your feet, you also ought to wash one another's feet. For I have given you an example, that you should do as I have done to you.

JOHN 13:14-15

One of the issues that most mattered to Jesus' disciples was who of them was the most favored and important to Him. In fact, two of the disciples, James and John, asked their mother to help them assume the seats of honor in Jesus' kingdom. Her request to Jesus was: "Grant that these two sons of mine may sit, one on Your right hand and the other on the left, in Your kingdom" (Matthew 20:21).

Jesus' response was that she didn't know what she was asking. She and her sons were interested in the trappings and benefits of power, but not the sacrifice. Otherwise, these sons of Zebedee could have been on Jesus' left and right when he prayed in the Garden (Matthew 26:40-46). Instead, they slept. They could have been on His left and right when He was arrested (Mark 14:50). Instead, they fled. They could have been on His left and right when he hung on a cross (Matthew 15:27, Luke 23:49, John 19:16-19, 26).   Instead, they stayed in the crowd.

When Jesus taught His disciples the true meaning of greatness, he taught with a towel and basin.   He washed their feet—the duty of a house servant.   Peter, still unable to comprehend the object lesson, initially refused to let Jesus lower Himself in such a way.

We live in a competitive and self-aggrandizing world. Examples of humility, kindness, helpfulness, and caring for others first—servanthood—are hard to find. As men, we are expected to be strong, bold leaders. God doesn't disagree with that, He just has a better way for you to lead—the way of the servant.

Great is the reward, the sense of purpose, the self satisfaction of one who follows the Master's example as a member of the "Towel and Basin Society."

Every man shall give as he is able, according to the blessing of the Lord your God which He has given you.

Deuteronomy 16:17

 REAL LIFE

Servant Heart, Servant Legs

AS TOLD TO DIANE H. PITTS

"I thought we were just helping; I didn't know Amber would be living with us the entire time." I wanted to help, but was reluctant to have someone else living in our home. Little did I know that God intended to use eighteen-year-old Amber Starr, a physically challenged orphan from Africa, to teach me much more than I could ever repay.

My wife, Tracey, told me Amber needed to stay with us for an extended period of time.

That might not sound overwhelming to you, but consider my situation: I'm Billy Duren, a solitary man surrounded by women. I already have six daughters. None of us knew what would be involved.

"Okay," I gulped. "Tell me more about her."

Amber had polio as a young child, rendering both legs almost completely useless. Her family, unable to care for her, asked the Good Shepherd's Fold orphanage to take her in. The director of the orphanage, himself physically challenged, urged Amber to stand with braces and crutches. She mastered that goal with extreme effort and was now in America for dangerous but needed spinal surgery.

In our home, Amber quickly lost guest privileges and became a Duren girl with chores and responsibilities. In actuality, we temporarily adopted her.

Some days were difficult. Amber's surgery was long and recuperation painful. We marveled at her patient suffering and determination, realizing how easy our lives were in comparison. During that time, Amber received notification that her father passed away. We supported her through the following weeks; loving those who mourn took on new meaning for me.

Months went by and soon Amber's time with us was nearing an end. One night she went with me to one of the concerts I promoted. She asked a simple question: "Have you ever thought of doing a concert for Good Shepherd's Fold to raise money for orphans?"

On a business trip to Dallas the next week, God spoke to me through her challenge. *To whom much is given, much is required. Will you take the gifts I've given you and serve Me in a different way?* That day, the idea for Mission Possible was born. We formed a volunteer vocal ensemble committed to sharing Amber's story and informing people about Good Shepherd's Fold Orphanage in Uganda. The ensemble members paid their own way to go on the road and put on concerts; all funds raised went to Good Shepherd's Fold. In two years, the Lord raised $10,000 for orphans as we depended on Him.

Amber's entire life was reliance on the Lord, and I learned through her example how God uses my dependence on Him to serve and help others. Amber had a service heart without service legs, and I had service legs without a servant's heart. She had the heart that prompted my actions to change forever.

ACTION STEP

VOLUNTEERISM IN AMERICA IS AT AN ALL-TIME LOW. THERE IS HUGE NEED FOR "BIG BROTHERS," TUTORS, SCOUT LEADERS, COACHES, AND OTHER FORMS OF MENTORING. ASK GOD IF HE HAS A SPECIFIC PLACE OF SERVICE FOR YOU IN YOUR CHURCH OR COMMUNITY.

PRAYER

Thank You, God, for sending Jesus into my life and heart with the gift of salvation. Help me to honor that gift through service to others.

EXPRESSING LOVE

IT'S NOT ENOUGH TO FEEL LOVE FOR THE SIGNIFICANT OTHERS IN OUR LIVES, WE MUST EXPRESS IT IN OUR WORDS AND ACTIONS.

Present your family and friends with their eulogies now—they won't be able to hear how much you love them and appreciate them from inside the coffin.

ANONYMOUS

TO THINK ABOUT

- Why does our society struggle so much to express affirmation and affection?
- Would your friends and family members describe you as warm and affirming, or cold and aloof?
- Are there some ways you can better express love to the important people in your life?

LESSON FOR LIFE

PROMISES:

God will—

Use you to build
up others
Ephesians 4:15-16

Perfect his love in you
1 John 4:12

Love others through you
1 Thessalonians 3:12

Searching for True Love

BIBLE STUDY PASSAGE: 1 JOHN 4

Do all these things; but most important, love each other.
Love is what holds you all together in perfect unity.

COLOSSIANS 3:14

There are a million songs on the airwaves that talk about love. But many of us don't feel very loved. Romance is woven into movies, TV shows, novels—even commercials—and yet there is far too little real affection among couples.

How do you do at expressing love to those significant others in your life? Children? Spouse? Neighbors? Extended family members?

Some reminders might be in order—

- *True love takes the initiative:* "In this is love, not that we loved God, but that He loved us and sent His Son to be the propitiation for our sins" (1 John 4:10 NKJV). God gave us the pattern for loving others: make the first move.
- *True love is active:* "My children, we should love people not only with words and talk, but by our actions and true caring" (1 John

3:18). Our culture obsesses over the emotions and romantic feelings of love. But true love is practical. If your neighbor is hungry, take them some food.

- True love is kind: "Love is not rude, is not selfish, and does not get upset with others" (1 Corinthians 13:5). Words may not be enough, but they still matter tremendously. When was the last time you said to your boss, "I appreciate you"? Do your children go to sleep with your final "I love you" of the day echoing in their hearts? Don't make people guess how you feel about them. Tell them!

- True love looks to the needs of others: "Do not be interested only in your own life, but be interested in the lives of others" (Philippians 2:4). All of us need affirmation in our own lives, too. But don't wait around to get what you need before you give others what they need. The good news is that God has a way of blessing you in greater measure than you bless others.

Share with your world the love that God has shared with you.

My children, we should love people not only with words and talk, but by our actions and true caring.

1 John 3:18

223

♥ REAL LIFE

Hugs

GARY STANLEY

My dad was a hugger. A gentle giant, he could put his arm around you and that simple act made the world a safer place. He always sensed when I needed to be enfolded in his arms—to know that I was safe and loved, that I belonged. He hugged me all the time.

Mom wasn't much of a hugger. My folks didn't fit the norm. His was the tender heart. Her heart was more carefully kept. Oh, she had a playful heart, taught dance, and was gifted in the bodily art of movement and grace. But she didn't understand the ways of hugging at the level Dad did. Her own dad had died during the influenza epidemic of 1919; she was two years old at the time (Aunt Judy was four, and Uncle John was only six days old). Daddy hugs aren't a part of her conscious memory. She's still learning how to translate all the love inside her into the embrace of a hug.

Dad initiated most of the hugs in our home.

I remember one day when Mom came home from work tired and frustrated. She was a first-grade teacher, and a room full of six-year-olds had "done her in." It was one of those days when she'd had no opportunity to get rid of the toxin of prolonged aggravation—you know, that feeling of being nibbled to death by ducks. Mom banged the cabinet doors and started to simmer something on the stove. Several things were coming to a rolling boil in the kitchen that afternoon.

Time to get out of the way, I thought.

Dad followed me downstairs and stood in the doorway. "Looks like thirty first graders have taken a toll on Mom today. I suspect we wouldn't have fared any better. Let's give her a hug!"

Dad was much more hopeful than I that a hug would help, so we marched upstairs to embrace a mother who didn't want to be embraced at that particular moment. He stepped into her personal space and unlocked the chains around her tense heart. To Mom's credit, she didn't bolt and bar the walls erected around her. She let Dad in, and the cares of the day began to dissipate like a static charge running down a grounding wire. It wasn't long before the three of us were in a group hug in the middle of the kitchen with our dog Waddles dancing around our feet.

It's been said that the best way to love a child is to love the child's mother. That day in the kitchen I was invited into a relationship that existed before I was born and that didn't depend on me. Of all the hugs I ever saw or got, the ones Dad gave Mom have meant the most. Knowing that people in my family loved each other and showed it made my home a safe place.

ACTION STEP

YOUR ASSIGNMENT FOR THIS SOUL MATTER IS SIMPLE. EVERY DAY FOR THE NEXT FIVE DAYS, YOU NEED TO—

- SAY "I LOVE YOU" TO FIVE DIFFERENT PEOPLE.
- HUG FIVE PEOPLE.

NOTE: IF YOU ARE GRIMACING AND FEELING HIGHLY RESISTANT, REALIZE THIS ACTIVITY HAS YOUR NAME ON IT!

PRAYER

Father, thank You for lavishing Your love on us with both words and amazing, incredible actions. Help me express love to the people in my life today.

CHURCH

WE ALL NEED A PLACE TO MEET WITH OTHERS WHO WILL HELP US GROW SPIRITUALLY.

God, having You for my Father is the best thing that could have ever happened in my life.   Thank You for letting me be in Your family.

JONI EARECKSON TADA

TO THINK ABOUT

- Why do you believe that church attendance patterns are down and that many who want to follow Jesus don't seem to value the need for church?
- What do you receive at church?   What do you give at church?
- Do you have an intentional meeting time each week dedicated to your spiritual growth?

LESSON FOR LIFE

PROMISES:

God will—

Minister to you
through others
1 Thessalonians 3:12
1Peter 4:10

Give you joy
through others
John 17:13

Teach you
through others
Colossians 3:16

Make you strong
through others
2 Thessalonians 2:17

Don't Quit Meeting

BIBLE STUDY PASSAGE: ACTS 4:23-35

You should not stay away from the church meetings, as some are doing, but you should meet together and encourage each other.   Do this even more as you see the day coming.

HEBREWS 10:25

Only about 20 percent of Americans now attend church weekly, though 40 percent attend with some regularity.

Is this a bad thing? Can't we get as much from a walk in the woods, like Emily Dickinson prescribed, as sitting in a pew? There are some things we can only get from meeting with other Christians—

- *Mutual encouragement:* "You should not stay away from the church meetings, as some are doing, but you should meet together and encourage each other" (Hebrews 10:25). It is dangerous to think that we don't need the encouragement and support of others who love God. Even if our relationship with God is fine, shouldn't we be there to encourage others?
- *Accountability:* "Fools think they are doing right, but the wise listen to

advice" (Proverbs 12:15). One of the downsides of our modern indi-
viduality is that without accountability, we get ourselves in trouble.
Maybe we are past the age when we have to tell Mom or Dad where
we are and when we'll be home—but sometimes that kept us out of
trouble. Sharing our lives with a circle of church friends can keep us
far from sin.

- The teaching of God's Word: "They spent their time learning the apos-
tles' teaching, sharing, breaking bread, and praying together" (Acts
2:42). Yes, it's very possible—and important—to grow in knowledge
of the Bible from individual study and reflection, but as the writer of
Proverbs tells us: "As iron sharpens iron, so people can improve each
other" (27:17). We need to interact on what God's Word really means
with others.
- Friendship: "This is my prayer for you: that your love will grow more
and more; that you will have knowledge and understanding with
your love" (Philippians 1:9). It is true that we are influenced by those
we spend significant time with. If all your significant relationships
are with people who don't support the lifestyle God wants for you,
you are putting yourself at risk.

People meeting together to worship, to pray, to study, to
encourage, to meet the needs of others—church is a great place to
experience those dynamics!

And I will give you shep-
herds according to My
heart, who will feed you
with knowledge and
understanding.
Jeremiah 3:15 NKJV

REAL LIFE

Be My Father, Daddy

TERRY HIGGINBOTHAM

When our first child was born, my wife had a difficult time delivering her. The doctors needed to do an emergency C-section—the baby's heart kept stopping.

As I heard, "Here she comes," I prayed my first prayer in nearly ten years: "Dear God, please don't let her die."

I had lost my need for God. When I was only thirteen, I had put my faith in a preacher. He turned out to be a man of God, but not a godly man. I blamed God for what happened to me, and I didn't trust church people.

Now, I found myself asking, "Sweetheart, what's the matter?" For thirteen years, Erin had been my reason. She was the only bright star in the dark sky that was my life.

"Nothing, Daddy," she sighed.

We had just moved. Erin had started making new friends and spent the night at a church lock-in with a girl named Raquel.

"Did you and Raquel have a fight?"

"No, just—"

"Just what?"

"Daddy, I was so embarrassed last night."

"Why?"

"I didn't know anything about the Bible."

"You do, too," I comforted. "You know about Adam and Eve. You know about Moses, Jonah, and all those others. You remember, from the book your grandma used to read you."

"Daddy, these guys were talking about how the Bible steered their life! They were talking about living by the Ten Commandments. Daddy, I couldn't even name them."

That night as I channel surfed, "What it means to be a father," registered in my mind. It was the ranting of a TV evangelist. As I half listened to his boisterous sermon, I thought about the men in my life. My father and grandfather had both been godly men. They had taught me well about honor, love, and faith. In that moment of clarity, I understood that the bad things that happened to me were not of God, but of man.

The next day, my neighbor, Jeff, invited us to go to his church. He said it was a different kind of place and that I would really like it. I accepted.

"Welcome to New Hope Church," yelled the young shepherd of this strange flock. It had been a while since I'd been in a church, and this one really was different. I'd never seen a coffee bar in a church foyer before. And I got the impression that about the only thing the jeans-clad congregants had in common was their desire to learn more about God.

By the end of the service, I knew that God had just ended my ten-year solitary journey. He knew He had to change my mind before He could change my heart. He also knew the only way to bring me back to the Church was through His star in my life, Erin.

That was four years ago. Today, I am Erin's father, not just her daddy. I am the spiritual leader of our house as God demands, and I can honestly say, "As for me and my house, we will serve the Lord." But the good things happening in our family would never have come if I hadn't taken my place in the family of God.

ACTION STEP

YOU MAY BE A GREAT CHURCH ATTENDEE, OR YOU MAY BE STRUGGLING TO GET THROUGH THE CHURCH DOORS ON A CONSISTENT BASIS. WHEREVER YOU ARE, DO SOMETHING THIS WEEK TO STEP UP YOUR GAME. FIND AN ACCOUNTABILITY GROUP AT YOUR CHURCH—OR FORM ONE WITH THREE OR FOUR OTHER GUYS. MAKE A COMMITMENT TO YOURSELF TO ATTEND SERVICE EVERY WEEK FOR TWO MONTHS, AND REWARD YOURSELF FOR MAKING GOOD ON YOUR GOAL. MAYBE RIGHT NOW YOU'RE NEEDING TO FIND A CHURCH— MAKE A PLAN TO VISIT A FEW CHURCHES OVER THE NEXT FEW SUNDAYS AND ASK GOD TO SHOW YOU WHERE TO PLUG IN.

TAKE COMFORT IN THE THOUGHT THAT YOUR LIFE WILL BECOME RICHER AS YOU SEEK GOD ALONGSIDE OTHERS.

PRAYER

Father God, please guide Your churches, and help me be a minister and be ministered to within my church.

PUTTING GOD FIRST

ONE OF THE GREATEST TRUTHS IN SCRIPTURE IS THAT ONLY WHEN WE GIVE OUR LIVES TO GOD DO WE LIVE WITH TRUE MEANING AND FULFILLMENT.

Just as a servant knows that he must first obey his master in all things, so the surrender to an implicit and unquestionable obedience must become the essential characteristic of our lives.

ANDREW MURRAY

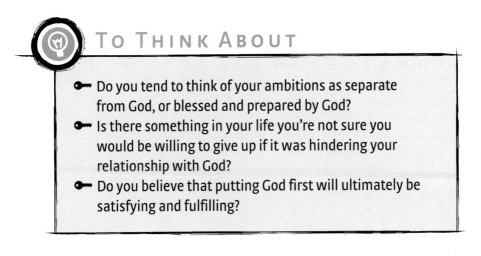

TO THINK ABOUT

- Do you tend to think of your ambitions as separate from God, or blessed and prepared by God?
- Is there something in your life you're not sure you would be willing to give up if it was hindering your relationship with God?
- Do you believe that putting God first will ultimately be satisfying and fulfilling?

LESSON FOR LIFE

PROMISES:

God will—

Give you rest as you
submit to Him
Matthew 11:29

Discipline you for your
ultimate good
Hebrews 12:10

Honor and reward your
obedience
Leviticus 18:5

First Things First

BIBLE STUDY PASSAGE: LUKE 10:38-42

But Martha was busy with all the work to be done. She went in and said, "Lord, don't you care that my sister has left me alone to do all the work? Tell her to help me."

LUKE 10:40

Have you ever found yourself in a situation of being so responsible, so dutiful, so correct in your religious practice that you lost your joy of knowing God?

In the famous parable of the lost son (Luke 15:11-32), a young man rejects his father's teachings and authority, demands his inheritance, and heads for a distant land where he squanders his financial and moral wealth. The loving father never gives up on this prodigal, and when his young son does come to his senses and ashamedly returns home, he welcomes him with open arms. He honors him with a feast, a party, a special cloak, and a golden ring. The older brother, who has faithfully stood by his father's side this whole time, is enraged that the prodigal should receive such a welcome. The father sadly reminds this older son that you don't have to work in a pig sty like his younger brother did to have a piggy attitude. Both sons learn about forgiveness and reconciliation from the love of their father.

In our study passage, we discover that Martha, much like the older brother, holds deep resentment toward a younger sibling. No, Mary is not immoral and rebellious, but she certainly doesn't have Martha's sense of responsibility. She leaves the dishes and chores to her sister so that she can sit at Jesus' feet. Wouldn't you feel a little resentful, too?

Jesus' answer to Martha's demand that He tell Mary to get busy is: "Martha, Martha, you are worried and upset about many things. Only one thing is important. Mary has chosen the better thing, and it will never be taken away from her" (vv. 41-42).

Is Jesus' point that we not set goals for our careers or spend time with family? Of course not. But He does remind us that the heart of our faith, our reason for living, is to love and worship God. Nothing else comes first!

Don't be stubborn as your ancestors were, but obey the Lord willingly. Come to the Temple, which he has made holy forever. Serve the Lord your God so he will not be angry with you.

2 Chronicles 30:8

REAL LIFE

Competing with God

ROLF GERRESSEN AS TOLD TO ESTHER M. BAILEY

When I married during my senior year of college, I started attending church. To my wife's dismay, however, I had no interest in becoming a Christian. I thought I told her ahead of time!

Until I was sixteen, I had been raised in Germany under a military influence. When I finished high school, I joined the United States Marines. I was tough, doing well in a teaching career, and didn't need God.

Hoping that the Holy Spirit would reach me through a powerful preacher, Charlene began to promote driving seventy miles to an evangelistic campaign.

Did I say promote? It was more like nagging. The campaign came up in every conversation until I finally agreed to go. I took my resentment with me and vowed not to listen.

To tune out the preacher, I took along papers to grade and books to read. Sitting a long way from the podium, I concentrated on my work. My wife was not happy, to say the least.

To this day I can't fully explain what happened. I barely listened to the message, but near the end of the sermon, my body began to tremble, my heart melted, and tears began to flow freely. I began the long journey to stand in front of the podium. The evangelist nodded at me before he gave the altar call. After following biblical instruction for salvation as presented to me, I received additional information to help me move forward on my spiritual journey.

After such a dramatic conversion, I should have jumped right in to serving God with my whole heart. I didn't. I wasn't yet willing to turn my life completely over to God. In my heart I knew my conversion was real, but it seemed my will was in competition with God's will. My mind that demanded logical proof couldn't quite step out on faith.

During my spiritual quest, God sent people into my life to help dispel my doubts. Some of my faith came from people in my past—the memory of a godly grandfather in Germany, a Sunday school teacher who demonstrated God's love, and even some of my buddies in the Marines. These were people whose lives made me hunger for something I didn't have—a trust and confidence in God.

The turning point in my pursuit of truth came when I started sitting under a Bible teacher like none I had ever known. He filled in all the missing pieces for me. As I learned about prophecy in the Old Testament that was fulfilled with the coming of Christ, my faith began to move forward.

Finally, I said, *Okay, God, You win! From now on You're in charge!* For more than half of my life I've given my personal ambitions to God. And He has brought me far more satisfaction than I could ever have achieved on my own.

ACTION STEP

FROM THE SIMPLE YELLOW WRISTBAND WITH THE WORD "STRENGTH" ON IT, TO A VARIETY OF OTHER COLORS AND REMINDERS, WE'VE REDISCOVERED THE POWER OF A SIMPLE PHYSICAL REMINDER. SEVERAL YEARS AGO, MILLIONS OF CHRISTIANS WORE WWJD WRIST BANDS TO RAISE THE QUESTION, WHAT WOULD JESUS DO? BEFORE MAKING CHOICES.

WHY NOT GET CREATIVE AND COME UP WITH YOUR OWN WRIST BAND? YOU CAN PUT MOST ANY PHRASE ON IT, BUT ONE THAT WOULD BE A GREAT REMINDER OF THIS SOUL MATTER IS: GOD FIRST.

PRAYER

Turn my heart and mind to You right now, O God, my kind and gracious Lord. I put You before all other goals, all other tasks.

HEALING FOR BROKENNESS

GOD CAN RESTORE EVEN THE MOST BROKEN OF LIVES.

If we only have the will to walk, then God is pleased with our stumbles.

C.S. LEWIS

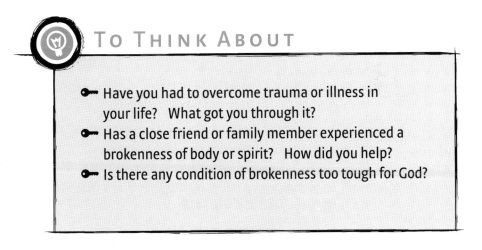

TO THINK ABOUT

- Have you had to overcome trauma or illness in your life? What got you through it?
- Has a close friend or family member experienced a brokenness of body or spirit? How did you help?
- Is there any condition of brokenness too tough for God?

LESSON FOR LIFE

PROMISES:

God will—
Heal and comfort you
Isaiah 35:10
Isaiah 57:19

Redeem you with love
and compassion
Psalm 103:4

Be merciful to you
Isaiah 49:13

Walk with you in your
darkest moments
Psalm 23:4

Wounded Healers

BIBLE STUDY PASSAGE: 1 CORINTHIANS 1:26-2:4

He comforts us every time we have trouble, so when others have trouble, we can comfort them with the same comfort God gives us.

2 CORINTHIANS 1:4

How could such a promising future go wrong so fast? All of us have witnessed instances when a friend or loved one has made bad choices—or through absolutely no choice of their own have simply been confronted with a tough set of circumstances—that have led to divorce, depression, alcoholism, a traumatic accident, a devastating illness.

The message of 2 Corinthians 1:3-6 is that there is hope for the broken. No life is filled with so much pain or in such a state of disarray that the God of all comfort cannot reach down with a healing touch. Some words of encouragement include—

• God never forsakes us (Hebrews 13:5): Even if our brokenness is of our own making, God is still kind and merciful, and always on our side. He is present in the midst of all circumstances.

- *God can turn tragedy into triumph (Psalm 30:11): Even in the darkest moments of the soul, God provides a supernatural comfort and perspective that allows individuals to experience and exhibit God's love and power. Martyrs have died with joy. The terminally ill have led others to experience God's love.*
- *God sends helpers (Galatians 6:10): Even though God is all-powerful and can intervene directly in healing, more often He sends human helpers, including doctors, to work on His behalf. It is no lack of faith to turn to others for help. It is a strong step of faith when we allow God to use us to minister to others.*
- *God heals all infirmities in eternity (1 Corinthians 15:42-43): Yes, God miraculously heals people today—but not in all cases. Paul gives the eternal perspective when he reminds us: "The sufferings we have now are nothing compared to the great glory that will be shown to us" (Romans 8:18). One day we will all exchange imperfect bodies for immortal bodies (Philippians 3:21). Heaven is a place where there are no more tears (Revelation 21:4).*

The blind see and the lame walk; the lepers are cleansed and the deaf hear; the dead are raised up and the poor have the gospel preached to them.

Matthew 11:5 NKJV

No human words or thoughts can explain away or provide comfort for certain kinds of suffering and pain. Maybe God doesn't want us to be able to do so. But His ultimate expression of comfort is the gift of salvation and eternal life through the death of His Son Jesus Christ (1 Peter 3:18).

REAL LIFE

Living Without Purpose

C. GRANT ENDICOTT

I sat in a hotel room, holding the phone with both hands in order to steady it against my face. How does a man tell his wife that he has been diagnosed with an illness he doesn't even understand?

I had just been diagnosed with Cyclothemia, a mild form of Bipolar Disorder.

My second call was to my pastor—who was also my boss. At first he was supportive, but when my diagnosis was determined by the church board to be a possible liability to the ministry, I was terminated.

Unfortunately, my wife's support soon dissolved as well. She simply couldn't accept the fact that I had an illness that could dramatically impact what she considered to be an ideal future, and we separated.

I wasn't worried about finding a job—I'd gotten lots of offers in the past. But no one in the ministry circles that I had served for the last twenty years wanted a man diagnosed with my illness, especially one who was soon to be divorced. I was a leper.

Six months after the diagnosis, I took the only offer I had received. I left my children and the only type of work I knew and began a new life as a technical writer for a company in Dallas, Texas.

I joined a large church and disappeared into the congregation. I missed my children desperately. Each day they were going to school, laughing and playing, and I didn't get to be there with them.

I begged my wife to reconcile, but she wouldn't budge. With every rejection, I became angrier and more deeply hurt—I was angry at her, the church leaders, even God. The hurt in my heart hardened until I was broken and dying inside.

Then, doctors found a blood clot in my spleen—I now had a blood-clotting disease to cope with in addition to everything else. During a routine scope of my stomach, I began to hemorrhage, putting me in a coma. My family was called and told not to expect me to live.

The Lord had other plans. The next seven months were trying—I was in the hospital more than I was home, enduring seemingly endless procedures and various tubes and needles inserted into my very tired body.

Once things settled down, I had time to think and I struggled desperately to determine my place in this world. Where could I possibly fit in God's plan? I was broken physically, mentally, and emotionally. I was divorced. Everything I used to think I was created to do—could I still do those things?

In the months that followed, I came to understand something: God loves me as I am—not for what I can do.

I'm not in ministry anymore, but I'm serving my church. I'm not the same father I used to be, but I still love and pray for my kids. I've learned that my purpose is not my vocation, but the way I yield myself to the Master for His glory. God's love has given me true purpose.

ACTION STEP

WHO ARE THE BROKEN IN OUR SOCIETY? MANY OF THEM CAN BE FOUND IN A VARIETY OF INSTITUTIONAL SETTINGS—HOMELESS SHELTERS, HOSPICES, NURSING HOMES, AND CORRECTIONAL FACILITIES. PLAN TO TOUR SEVERAL FACILITIES AS AN EDUCATIONAL PROCESS. BUT ALONG THE WAY, ASK GOD TO SPEAK TO YOUR HEART ABOUT FINDING A PLACE OF VOLUNTEER SERVICE.

PRAYER

Father, thank You for healing us and redeeming us. Thank You for strength in the midst of difficulty. Help me cling to your love and power today. Amen.

A PRAYER FOR YOUR SOUL

The most important soul matter, of course, is having a relationship with God. Everything in our lives-everything in our entire existence-has new, eternal meaning when we understand that God loves us and has made a way to save us through Jesus Christ. All of this may be new to you. If you'd like to know that you have a lasting relationship with God through Jesus, pray this prayer:

Heavenly Father, I come to You admitting that I am a sinner. I believe that Your Son, Jesus, died on the cross and rose from the dead to take away my sins. Jesus, I choose to follow You and ask that You fill me with the Holy Spirit so that I can understand more about You. Thank You for adopting me, and thank You that I am now a child of God. Amen.

HOW TO READ AND STUDY THE BIBLE

One of the most important keys to nurturing your soul is consistent reading and studying of Scripture. If you're a new Bible reader, be patient with yourself! Learn to study and apply God's Word one step at a time.

1. **Have your own Bible.** *Your own Bible is the one that has your name in it, the one that you not only carry to church, but even remember to bring home with you. You need a Bible that you cherish and keep close at hand.*

2. **Begin with prayer.** *Every time you sit down to read your Bible, ask God to speak to you through Scripture. Let Him know you are ready and willing to hear His voice.*

3. **Plan a Bible-reading schedule.** *You will profit more from Bible reading if you study entire books at a time, not just parts here and there. So map out a good Bible-reading schedule, planning which books to work through several at a time.*

4. **Use a study method.** *Discipline in Bible study is just like discipline in any other area—discipline leads to positive and healthy experiences in our lives.*

If you keep a notebook or prayer journal, you might start a section titled "My Time in the Word." As you learn one simple Bible study method, you'll see how a notebook can be used to make your time in the Word more effective.

Step One:

LOOK FOR THE BIG PICTURE

Before focusing on several verses of a particular chapter, get an overall idea of the book you are reading. Try to find out who is writing the book, to whom, and why. Many Bibles contain a short introduction to each book of the Bible with a lot of this information given. Another way to do this is to read the entire book quickly; if it is a longer book, simply skim through it and note the paragraph headings printed in your Bible. You're not trying to read every word, just get acquainted with the flow and feeling of the book.

Step Two:

SELECT A STUDY PASSAGE

Once you have an idea of the big picture, you'll want to study the entire book in chunks—anywhere from a few verses to an entire chapter at a time.

When you study a passage, what counts is quality of reading, not quantity. One caution: You will not want to break up paragraphs, or you will lose the writer's train of thought.

Step Three:

READ THE STUDY PASSAGE SEVERAL TIMES

After you choose the verses you are going to study, read that section of Scripture at least two times. Three or four times would be better. And remember, you set the pace—you can choose to study a chapter or just a few verses. What counts is that you grow in an understanding of God's Word.

Step Four:

SEARCH FOR MAJOR TRUTHS

As you read through your study passage for the third or fourth time, note the key thoughts found there. What does the writer want the people who read this to understand? Look for commands to be obeyed, warnings to be heeded, promises to be claimed, and truths to be believed.

Set aside a space in your journal for you to jot down these key thoughts and major truths.

Step Five:

ASK QUESTIONS

Now is the time to raise questions that come to your mind. Not everything in Scripture is immediately or easily understood. Do not be surprised or intimidated by this fact.

Write down your questions in your notebook or journal. Here are several places where you can go to get answers to these questions.

• **Scripture:** Use a concordance or study Bible to look up passages of Scripture that deal with the subject you're studying—often, one scripture can help explain another.

• **Commentaries:** Commentaries study and explain Bible passages a little at a time. Your church library probably contains several sets of commentaries you could borrow.

• **Pastors and teachers:** Your pastor and Sunday school teachers may not be able to give you an answer right away, but they will be willing to search for answers with you.

Step Six:

PUTTING IT INTO PRACTICE

You need to apply the Bible to your life now. "Do not merely listen to the word ... Do what it says" (1:22, italics added) was James' advice.

Is there something you are doing that you shouldn't be doing? Is there something you are not doing that you need to be doing? Is there something about God or Jesus or the Holy Spirit that you did not know before? Do you need to be more sensitive to someone at work? Do you need to seek someone's forgiveness? Do you need to forgive someone?

Step Seven:

NOTE A VERSE TO REMEMBER

The final step in your Bible study is to take one last look at your study passage and write down a verse or two that you want to remember most. Memorizing scripture is a terrific discipline. It allows you to take scripture with you, even when you don't or can't have your Bible at hand.

Writing out a key verse will make remembering it much easier for you. It is a good start to memorizing it also.

May God cause your soul to stretch and grow
as you embark on a journey through His Word!

Acknowledgements

"Wannabe Lance Armstrong: A Real Winner" © Katherine Crawford. Used by permission. All rights reserved.

"Seeking Forward Motion" © Ken Clifton. Used by permission. All rights reserved.

"Nightmare" © Nanette Thorsen-Snipes. Used by permission. All rights reserved.

"Still Skiing" © Glenda Palmer. Used by permission. All rights reserved.

"My Rebel" © Nanette Thorsen-Snipes. Used by permission. All rights reserved.

"Am I My Brother's Keeper?" © Karen Kilby. Used by permission. All rights reserved.

"Easy Lover" © Jay Cookingham. Used by permission. All rights reserved.

"Lesson from Desert Storm" © Kayleen Reusser. Used by permission. All rights reserved.

"You Da Man!" © Nanette Thorsen-Snipes. Used by permission. All rights reserved.

"Vaya Con Dios" © Terry Higginbotham. Used by permission. All rights reserved.

"My Life as a Reluctant Bus Driver" © Jessica Inman. Used by permission. All rights reserved.

"A Real Creep" © Orvey Hampton. Used by permission. All rights reserved.

"Happy Thanksgiving" © Jay Cookingham. Used by permission. All rights reserved.

"'Dad, I'll Always Love You'" © Joan Clayton. Used by permission. All rights reserved.

"Staying the Course" © Jessica Inman. Used by permission. All rights reserved.

"The Power of a Confession" © Larry Miller. Used by permission. All rights reserved.

"A True Hope" © Jerry Lane. Used by permission. All rights reserved.

"Server of Blessings" © Ginger Cox. Used by permission. All rights reserved.

"The Nail" © Max Davis. Used by permission. All rights reserved.

"Facing the Thing I Fear" © Terry Burns. Used by permission. All rights reserved.

"My Beautiful Long Hair" © LaRose Karr. Used by permission. All rights reserved.

"Billy's Pecan Pie" © Karen Kilby. Used by permission. All rights reserved.

"Some Things Only God Can Do" © Jennifer Johnson. Used by permission. All rights reserved.

"Living My Dream" © Elaine Young McGuire. Used by permission. All rights reserved.

"Loud and Clear" © Jay Cookingham. Used by permission. All rights reserved.

"By the Grace of God" © Max Davis. From *Desperate Dependence*, published 2004.
     Used by permission of Cook Communications Ministries.

"Integrity's Reward" © Esther M. Bailey. Used by permission. All rights reserved.

"Leaving My Anger Behind" © LaRose Karr. Used by permission. All rights reserved.

"Jim" © David Flanagan. Used by permission. All rights reserved.

"From Darkness to Light" © Nanette Thorsen-Snipes. Used by permission. All rights reserved.

"Pastures of Hope" © rondi Feyereisen. Used by permission. All rights reserved.

"Saving Jael" © C. Hope Flinchbaugh. Used by permission. All rights reserved.

"Family Resemblance" © Jay Cookingham. Used by permission. All rights reserved.

"God Is Never Late" © Stan Toler. From *God Is Never Late; He's Seldom Early; He's Always Right on Time*,
     published 2004. Used by permission of Beacon Hill Press.

"Servant Heart, Servant Legs" © Diane H. Pitts. Used by permission. All rights reserved.

"Hugs" © Gary Stanley. From *How to Make a Moose Run*, published 2001.
     Used by permission of Cook Communications Ministries.

"Be My Father, Daddy" © Terry Higginbotham. Used by permission. All rights reserved.

"Competing with God" © Esther M. Bailey. Used by permission. All rights reserved.

"Living without Purpose" © C. Grant Endicott. Used by permission. All rights reserved.

Your Story

Has there been a time in your life when you encoun-tered God in a powerful way that changed and enriched your soul? Would your story encourage others to grow closer to God and improve their lives?

WE WOULD LOVE TO CONSIDER YOUR STORY FOR FUTURE EDITIONS OF SOUL MATTERS. PLEASE SHARE YOUR STORY TODAY, WON'T YOU? FOR WRITER'S GUIDELINES, UPCOMING TITLES, AND SUBMISSION PROCEDURES, VISIT:

www.soulmattersbooks.com

Or send a postage-paid, self-addressed envelope to:

**Mark Gilroy Communications, Inc.
6528 E. 101st Street, Suite 416
Tulsa, Oklahoma 74133-6754**